The Cop Doc's
Classic Writings on Police Careers

Part of

The Cop Doc's Classic Writings
Series of Books

First Edition

Manufactured in the United States of America

ISBN: 978-0-9828697-0-3
(6X9 US trade paperback)

www.TheCopDoc.com

The Cop Doc's
Classic Writings on Police Careers

Part of

The Cop Doc's Classic Writings
Series of Books

By

Former Police Chief & Police Academy Director
Dr. Richard Weinblatt
The Cop Doc

Also by

Dr. Richard Weinblatt

Books

Reserve Law Enforcement in the United States:
A National Study of State, County, and City Standards
Concerning the Training & Numbers of Non-full-time
Police and Sheriff's Personnel (1993)

The Cop Doc's Classic Writings on
Police Media Relations (2010)

Columns

. Law and Order:
The Magazine for Police Management
"Reserve Reports"
(1991-2001)

Officer.com
"Reserve Power" and "Career Corner"
(2005-2006)

PoliceLink.com
"Law Enforcement Career Expert"
(2007-Present)

PoliceOne.com
"Weinblatt's Tips" and "Police and the Press"
(2004-Present)

About the Author

Dr. Richard Weinblatt, The Cop Doc, is a law enforcement expert, consultant, writer, radio show host, and media commentator, who has served as a police chief, criminal justice professor, and police academy director. He has worked in several regions of the United States in reserve and full-time sworn positions ranging from auxiliary police lieutenant in New Jersey to Patrol Division Deputy Sheriff in New Mexico to Police Chief in North Carolina.

A certified instructor for Taser, pepper spray, baton, firearms, vehicle operations, and defensive tactics, Dr. Weinblatt instructed and/or oversaw criminal justice degree programs and police academies in Florida, New Mexico, North Carolina, and Ohio.

A well-known police issues commentator for local and national media, Dr. Weinblatt has been interviewed by the Associated Press, CBS News, CNN, HLN, MSNBC, and The Washington Post among others. He has authored hundreds of articles on law enforcement topics for magazines and websites

Dr. Weinblatt earned a bachelor's degree in Administration of Justice, a Master of Public Administration in Criminal Justice, an Education Specialist degree and a Doctor of Education.

Dr. Weinblatt resides in the greater Orlando, FL, area with his wife, Anne, and son, Michael. Further information is available at www.TheCopDoc.com.

Dedication

This book is dedicated to the men and women who pin on a badge and believe in honor and integrity. They engage in a difficult profession on a daily basis and advance forward when others retreat.

This book on police career issues is also dedicated to the people who aspire to walk in all the honorable law enforcers' footsteps.

Acknowledgements

As with any author's book, many people are involved either directly or indirectly in helping the massive project come to fruition. This book was no different.

The genesis of the material for this particular book in The Cop Doc's Classic Writings series (as well as others in the series) came from the gurus, past and present, of the big law enforcement magazines and websites.

The list of them is long, but mention is certainly warranted of the following individuals that gave the green light to originally publishing these writings: American Police Beat's Cynthia Brown, Corrections Technology & Management's Tim Burke, Law and Order: The Magazine for Police Management's Bruce W. Cameron and Ed Sanow, Officer.com's Tim Dees, Police: The Law Enforcement Magazine's Randall C. Resch and Dennis Hall, PoliceLink.com's Chris Cosgriff and Kevin Powers, and PoliceOne.com's Scott Buhrmaster and Doug Wyllie.

Special attention is accorded to Bruce W. Cameron, the Editor Emeritus of Law and Order: The Magazine for Police Management, as he was the impetus for the writing endeavors back in 1989.

Also of invaluable assistance was the family: Anne, the wifey, and Michael, the munchkin.

Contents

Dr. Richard Weinblatt

The Cop Doc's
Classic Writings on Police Careers

Introduction

As a person who has been on both sides of the law enforcement career hiring and promotion process (position candidate and assessor), I have been fortunate enough to be able to share information that I have learned with others who aspire to enter the police services field and eventually seek to become trainers, educators, or even police chiefs. For years I have answered questions and those queries have only intensified over time.

One of the main ways that I have been able to get the information and advice out to quench the thirst for information about the most misunderstood of professions is by having written hundreds of articles since 1989. In addition to articles on law enforcement career issues, I have also written on other police topics such as tactical issues, media relations, and leadership.

I appreciate those many editors for their faith in my writing (and for their checks over the years so they could secure the first time publication rights). The articles have appeared in respected outlets including American Police Beat, Corrections Technology & Management, Law and Order: The Magazine for Police Management, Law Officer Magazine, Officer.com, PoliceOne.com, PoliceLink.com, Police: The Law Officer's Magazine, and Sheriff Magazine, among others.

The Cop Doc's Classic Writings on Police Careers book is a compilation of articles on law enforcement career issues. It is part of a series of books sharing my classic writings on law enforcement topics. While the writings span over two decades, the information contained therein are as applicable today as when they were originally typed.

This book is designed to capture information that I had presented before in response to people's curiosity, but is no less valid in today's competitive world. If anything, I have seen the requests for career information ratchet up dramatically with the downturn in the economy.

The aim here is to help with the issues that span a broad police career spectrum. That includes the young man or woman who is contemplating how to successfully enter a career in law enforcement and the parent wondering how to advise them on what they need to do to succeed. It also encompasses the veteran law enforcer facing a promotion board to gain rank or a selection process for police chief, as well as for the crime fighter looking to switch over to being a police academy instructor or criminal justice professor.

Indeed, many of the tips, suggestions, and concepts presented within these pages apply far beyond the scope of policing and extend into other areas of public and non-profit service, as well as the private sector.

It is my fervent hope that these timeless writings help you to reach your dreams and make your hopes come true.

Dr. Richard Weinblatt
The Cop Doc
Orlando, FL

www.TheCopDoc.com

Spring 1993
The F.O.P. Journal

Reserve Policing: Stepping Stone to a Career

Ryan T. Kane views his work as an auxiliary police officer in South Brunswick Township, NJ, as more than just a sideline activity. The 20-year-old criminal justice student is actively experiencing, through his volunteer law enforcer stints, what his future might look like as a full-time officer.

"We expect to have about eight auxiliaries apply for our openings," said South Brunswick Police Captain Frederick A. Thompson. The holder of a master's degree, Thompson, like other progressive police executives, has identified in-house reserve forces as a testing ground of sorts for future full-time employees.

Kane, who is a certified Monadnock PR-24 sidehandle baton instructor, represents one of the two large segments that make up the nation's 250,000 reserve law enforcement component. Volunteer or part-time police officers have long used their service as a stepping stone reflective of their career aspirations. The other segment of reservists is successful members of the community who give back to society through their service.

Sometimes called auxiliary or special officers, reserves in most jurisdictions have to overcome similar or identical screening and training challenges as those confronting regular officers. Many have had the same state certifications as full-timers and cross over to salaried status without having to go back through a police academy again.

Many administrators gravitate to the concept as it allows them to see how prospective officers react, sometimes quite literally under fire. "We encourage our auxiliaries to pursue a career. We know what they can do as we've watched them in action in uniform already," Thompson said.

Providing the basis of any good reserve springboard is a bona fide police training regime. Reserves in North Carolina must meet the same minimum training standards and thus find themselves using their certification when they go full-time. In the Tar Heel State, reserve and full-time deputy sheriffs undergo 444 hours of academy training whereas reserve and full-time police officers get 432 hours. The distinction is made police versus sheriff; not reserve status as opposed to salaried occupation.

In a similar vein, the Georgia Peace Officer Standards and Training Council's Jim Sims said that their attorney general has said, "If it walks like a duck, it must be a duck." The state makes no distinction between paid, part-time or volunteer officers provided they are 280-hour fully POST certified.

In the shadow of New York City, special police officers in Greenwich, CT, also go through an identical screening and training process. The training is the standardized 498 hour Connecticut Municipal Police Training Council (CMPTC) mandated curriculum. The difference manifests itself only in the scheduling as the training is conducted at night and on the weekends for a longer period of time.

The convenience of an identical academy scheduled for reserves does not go unnoticed by salaried personnel. In Memphis, TN, the current 430-hour Shelby County Sheriff's Office Reserve Academy, identical to the full-time day academy, boasts 16 newly minted regular law enforcers as students.

Chief B.J. Patterson, director of the reserve deputy sheriff program, said the uniforms, badges and identification cards are identical for the reserves. It makes sense to them that the training is on an equal par and is therefore attractive to all facets of law enforcement.

The Ramsey County, MN Sheriff's Department takes the concept of reserve to full-time one step further. The reserve program, based out of their Shoreview offices, is mostly comprised of criminal justice students who are using their service as a stepping stone into a full-time career. Of the 70 reserves, 40 have earned their 400-hour Minnesota- state license and are therefore carrying Glock Model 17 firearms and are solo qualified. The remaining 30 non-licensed reserve deputies must have 36 hours of pre-service training and they patrol unarmed under the watchful eyes of a certified officer. Once again, the entry standards are rigorous, mirroring the full-time standards, and include MMPI psychological testing, and drug screening.

"We go through the same training and are fully state-certified police officers," said Special Sergeant Eric Omdahl, Greenwich's top volunteer cop, who added that his officers have the legal right to carry firearms off duty.

Departments from Anchorage to Honolulu utilize the same entrance standards for reserves as they do for full timers. In most cases, the screening elements include a written test, background investigation, oral interview, psychological testing, physical agility test, medical exam, drug urinalysis and a polygraph test.

Over in Boise, ID, one of the nation's fastest growing regions, Jim Fox, the deputy sheriff who oversees the Ada County Sheriff's Office's Reserve Deputy Program, said their biggest problem is the exodus of volunteers to full-time law enforcement slots. "We screen these people as we do for regular deputies," explained Fox. "They have to go through a written test, oral interview, physical assessment and final interview."

Once past the entrance and training phases, the experience gained though actual work in the field proves invaluable to aspiring full-timers. Becoming a working reserve allows the young adult to separate fact from fiction often portrayed on television. Being a police officer becomes real.

"Someone who has worked for us as an auxiliary officer and is experienced knows this is the career for them," said Thompson.

The experience South Brunswick's Kane has garnered through his service as a volunteer police officer has not only given administrators a peek at his abilities, but has also given him an insight into himself. "After being involved in my first foot chase, I feel confident I can do the job," said Kane recalling one of many eventful evenings on patrol. In-service training ensures that the reservists stay up on the latest police procedures and equipment. Theories and intangible concepts become concrete when merged with the sights and sounds of the streets of justice.

Ada County requires that eight hours be spent on in-service training each month. The figure does not include patrol or other reserve duties. The South Brunswick Police Department was the first agency in New Jersey to acquire an in-car computer mobile data terminal system, a policing tool Kane is now thoroughly familiar with.

The 71 auxiliary state troopers with the Vermont State Police, one of eight state police/highway patrol agencies that utilize reserve troopers, work extensively in marine enforcement and worked 13,000 hours last year in that area alone. In addition to their state police academy stint, they even get two days of training with the U.S. Coast Guard on marine issues.

Service in reserve law enforcement provides administrators a viable pool of talent from which to draw. The lower cost of identifying those who may be "badge and gun happy" is facilitated by closely supervising volunteer or part-time personnel. On the other side of the desk, the young officers themselves are afforded an opportunity to assess the viability of police work as a career choice.

September 1994
Law and Order:
The Magazine for Police Management

Oral Boards Go High-Tech

B-PAD, Behavioral Personnel Assessment Device, is growing popularity as law enforcement agencies search for recruits. But many police administrators are still unfamiliar with these programs so it is worth a look at how successful they are.

Scenario #1: Dispatched as back up to a closed store with an open door, you find a fellow officer stealing an inexpensive piece of merchandise.

Scenario #2: You enter the open door of a biracial couple's home to find them both yelling profanities at each other and both showing signs of recent physical abuse.

B-PAD candidates are seated in front of a monitor and watch eight scenarios, such as the ones above, unfold on the screen. At the end of each scenario, the word "respond" appears and the candidate, who is alone in the room and is being taped by a camera located to the right of the monitor, has 45 seconds in which to verbally give his or her response to the situation. Raters from the hiring agency, trained by the folks from the Napa, CA, B-PAD Group, Inc., examine the tapes and issue a grade based on uniform criteria.

A 21st century approach using standardized professionally produced video scenarios depicting "like circumstances" is a rapidly-growing trend that answers many of the concerns of traditional assessment testing. A group in California, comprised of five police psychologists, believes that they have the answer to the problems that ail time-consuming, expensive, non-standardized and non-validated traditional oral boards and role-playing assessment centers.

The idea is B-PAD, and it now involves 58 agencies in 16 states. The originators of the concept claim 1,360 applicants have gone through and have anonymously sent in their comments with "no adverse impact reported."

"Our oral boards stretched over a two week period and we were paying overtime rate for board members to complete their work," recalled Tim Reeves, undersheriff of the 85 sworn full-time deputy Dona Ana County Sheriff's Office, the first agency in New Mexico to utilize B-PAD. "With the B-PAD method, we need only one day for raters to review the tapes and we can schedule that day at our convenience."

Dona Ana County Sheriff's Captain Jerry Little, speaking from his office in Las Cruces, NM, said that 103 people aspiring to be deputy sheriffs started out in their recent hiring tests. Six remained at the end of the process. "It would have taken much longer using an oral board to handle those who passed the written and physical assessments," Little said.

Instead of spending money on personnel to run two weeks of oral boards, Dona Ana County paid a one-time fee of $3,500 and completed the task in one day.

Dr. David Corey, co-founder of the B-PAD Group, said the usual one-time fee ranges from $2,900 to $6,900, "depending on the size of the agency and whether the training is done at the agency or at the B-PAD Group in California." Departments pay additional per applicant fees only if they want Corey's people to continue monitoring the agency's test raters to insure that no bias takes place.

"The B-PAD people site-trained out agency's raters," Reeves said in expressing his satisfaction with the way the training unfolded. "They were professional and more in depth than we expected."

While the majority of the police departments on B-PAD's customer list are large organizations like Austin, TX, Honolulu, HI, Maricopa County, AZ, and San Francisco International Airport, smaller agencies have also discovered the benefits of B-PAD video testing. According to Corey, agencies are banding together in a consortium arrangement to make their services affordable.

With ten sworn officers, the Sutherlin Police Department located in the southwest quadrant of Oregon thought they couldn't find any money in last year's $525,584 budget to conduct B-PAD. At least not if they went in alone. Located two hours south of Portland, OR, the department used B-PAD to hire two officers out of an initial field of 20.

"Alone, the cost was prohibitive, so we joined with the Douglas County (OR) Sheriff's Office," Sutherlin's Lieutenant Richard Schwartz reported, "While saving us a lot of money, this gives us feedback and weeds out problem people. We do it in place of an oral interview board."

Dona Ana County's Little, whose southern New Mexican agency covers 4,000 square miles including 50 miles along the Mexican border, said the B-PAD method removes the problems of "questions branching off into other questions" which happens at traditional oral boards. He said B-PAD removes elements of favoritism and bias, "as everyone gets the same stimulus to react and everyone is graded the same..." An additional advantage is the ability to save the tapes which document the candidates' performance.

Corey said the developers avoided designing a video instrument that "branches like an oral board or the firearms training simulator, which is more appropriate for training." By avoiding such divergent situations, he said the test avoids being thrown out due to non-standardization.

Corey finds it ironic that governmental personnel offices ask for validity studies on B-PAD, which the B-PAD Group folks provide, yet the governmental administrators don't have similar data in their files for traditional oral boards. "This is a far more defensible test than the oral board," Corey stated.

Reeves said administrators are looking for credible standards on which to base their hiring decisions. He said that since there are validated and standardized written tests on the market, it makes sense that the same criteria can be successfully applied to this high-tech version of an oral board.

The cost factor associated with this method of testing vs. traditional oral boards was what sparked initial interest on the part of many agencies who have become believers. As happened with the Dona Ana County Sheriff's Office, personnel involved in the evaluation of candidates put in fewer working hours, thereby lowering a major cost in the process.

Dr. Tom Hickey, police psychologist with the Memphis, TN, Police Department since 1977, said B-PAD has saved them time and money and is very efficient. The 1,417 sworn officer agency is planning to use B-PAD for promotions, another package offered by the B-PAD

Group (they also offer corrections and fire service versions).

"We had 600 (applicants) overall and, after background checks, ran 350 people through the process," Hickey said. "We ranked them and made job offers to the top 30."

The 80 sworn officer Merced, CA, Police Department has put 200 candidates through B-PAD to validate other instruments in their two recent hiring periods which took place over the course of a nine month span. "In my opinion, one of the most valuable tools in the police hiring process is a thorough background investigation," Patrick N. Lunney, police chief of the Merced force said. "Unfortunately, with the volumes of people going for police jobs, it can become costly."

Lunney explained that for their last testing process, they had 500 people initially. He lamented that knocking out even half, 250, is still too large a number for an agency his size to handle in the background phase.

Reeves, who has done graduate work in public administration, pointed out since they spend upwards of $10,000 to train a law enforcer in New Mexico, it makes sense to eliminate unlikely candidates prior to incurring the expense.

With seven years in the Marine Corps., Anthony Russell has had his share of military- style oral boards. The newly hired Memphis police officer went through B-PAD recently as part of the city's hiring process and proclaimed it "as stressful" as traditional oral examinations. "You just have to do your natural way to react to a situation," Russell said.

Russell, who had not served in any other law enforcement capacity, said he thinks the B-PAD gave a "realistic assessment'" of how he would act as a police officer. While he enjoyed the experience, he admitted he did not like sitting in a room by himself and talking to a monitor, microphone, and TV camera.

That the tape does not provide feedback is a common complaint, but the lack of positive or negative feedback could be advantageous. "As we all know, the most difficult person an officer runs into on the street is a non-responsive person," Corey said.

"Being a good actor in front of the camera and doing well in B-PAD may be connected," Corey conceded on a related point. "But that skill is used in law enforcement in general. You must pretend to be in control when you may not be. You must pretend not to be frightened when you may be."

From time to time we all play a role, echoed Memphis' Hickey. "Having the ability to sell yourself and relate to others is inherent in most jobs and certainly is the case in police work."

Reeves said that Dona Ana County "looks for a high level of interpersonal skills in today's cops." He said they want deputy sheriffs to be verbally firm, yet retrained with regard to force. He said B-PAD gives them an economical way to determine that quality.

"Oral review boards don't usually wipe out that many people," pointed out Reeves who has also been in law enforcement in Hawaii. "We eliminated 55% of the people who made it to the B-PAD. To drop a problem officer out later may be at the expensive cost of a lawsuit."

Merced's Lunney, noting that there is probably some awareness of the camera with B-PAD, pointed out that the problem of a good actor is also present in traditional oral boards. Lunney's agency is unusual in that those few that make it through B-PAD appear in front of an oral board where the candidate "can discuss or clarify for the board responses to the B-PAD."

"B-PAD is valuable, but we need to recognize its limitations and strengths," Lunney said. "It is a nice addition to backgrounds and other parts of the process."

"In a less-than-perfect world where humans judge other humans to determine if they are capable of making life and death decisions, Reeves said B-PAD helps them to weed out potential problems in a cost efficient manner.

Mirroring the sentiments of many other law enforcement executives regarding the responsibility which rests on their shoulders, Reeves said that they just don't have the time to spend with the many applicants who want to become sworn officers. He said B-PAD makes the process much more manageable. "The time we are able to spend with an applicant today is almost non-existent. We'd better make it count."

March 1997
American Police Beat

The paychecks are high and so is morale

Members of the Suffolk County Police Department have long been the envy of law enforcement officers around the country.

Although there are departments that reportedly are higher paid, the substantial pay checks brought home by officers in Suffolk and nearby Nassau County Police Departments have received the most attention.

Although the grass may seem greener in a department where patrol officers can top out at $59,541 a year and the union was just successful in gaining a raise of 18.6 percent over the next four years, there is more to the story than just the bottom line.

"Sure other officers are envious of our pay here," explains Recruitment Sergeant Ken Williams. "But there's a reason for it."

Williams notes that homes in Suffolk County, an affluent suburb only 20 miles east of New York City, are among the highest priced in the nation. "We have one of the highest costs of living," Williams says. "and we also have an affluent community that has the ability and desire to pay the taxes to support its police."

While Suffolk cops may earn more than most of their colleagues around the country, they also have some extraordinary demands placed on them. "When a Suffolk County officer graduates from the police academy, they are a fully qualified EMT as well," explains Williams. "In most departments EMTs are a completely separate position.

And Suffolk County cops are busy. In 1995, officers handled 685,840 calls for service and there were 1,042895 calls to the 911 system. Most Suffolk officers work one-man cars. Only eight percent of the units are manned by two officers.

Comprised of 2,757 full-time personnel spread out among seven precincts (seven more are in the works), Suffolk cops police a 926 square mile, 1.4 million population county.

The last written test given on June 8th had 34,330 attendees who each forked over a $50 application fee.

"Over 100 of those test takers got 100 percent," Williams adds. "We expect to hire around 400 during the life of the list."

Following the written exam, aspiring Suffolk County fuzz take the gender and age specific physical assessment test based on the Cooper Institute Standards. A psychological, medical and background investigation including a polygraph follows.

Sgt. Williams notes that although the last academy class had 10 cadets with former law enforcement experience, the famed drain of New York City officers over to Suffolk County is largely a myth. At the very most, former New York cops never make up more than ten percent of any of our academy classes," Williams said.

The Suffolk County academy runs 28 weeks and all must attend the day operation regardless of previous training. The subsequent field training runs for 12 weeks with probation starting the first day of the academy and lasting 18 months.

The "two tour" system has the officers working 232 days a year (the average worker in the U.S. plies his or her trade 260 days per annum).

The steady ten hour midnight shift (10:00 pm to 8:00 am) is the first assignment with four days on and four days off.

With seniority, the other option becomes readily available with five days on and four days off rotating the 4:00 pm to midnight and 8:00 am to 4:00 pm shifts once a week.

The agency usually pays around half the officers' tuition (with a "C" average or better).

Although only a high school diploma is required for applicants, 48 percent of the Suffolk County force has college degrees. In addition there are 78 officers with Master's degrees and at least ten sworn officers who are attorneys.

The academy wage is $34,617 a year and is upped to $36,617.

The one year anniversary mark sees $41,445 and steady increases each year for the next four years finds an officer topping out at $59.541. Add onto those figures a midnight shift differential of $6,254 and the swing/day shift differential of $2,977. All of the numbers have just been renegotiated with the officers' union and will climb 18.6 percent over the next four years.

Those serving in units such as the dive team, emergency services, and aviation (they have four helicopters) get an additional hazardous duty pay of around $3,000 per annum.

The sergeant's base pay comes in at $74,105. Sergeant (available after a minimum of three years), lieutenant, and captain positions are civil service tested posts. Higher ranks are appointed by the police commissioner.

Most officers serve in patrol for five years before becoming eligible for promotion unless they have special prior experience or training.

Dr. Richard Weinblatt

October 1997
Police:
The Law Enforcement Magazine

So... You Wanna' Be a Police Chief

Long the goal of many a beat officer, the coveted title of police chief is for many, synonymous with power, respect and stature within the community. However, pinning on the chief's badge and donning the scrambled egg-laden hat may not be an assignment as easily garnered or held as it once was. Today, it's an even more complex political, fiscal, legal and social arena that a police chief must operate in.

"Like the police officer's job has changed, so too has that of the police chief," said Frankfort, IL, Police Chief Darrell L. Sanders, who also serves as president of the respected 15,803 member-strong International Association of Chiefs of Police (IACP). He enumerated such complex situations as collective bargaining and litigious endeavors which add to the stress of the job.

"The expectations are higher and people are always looking for 'what have you done for me lately,'" he told POLICE.

"Some police officers have a good idea of what the job entails, but others don't," echoed Joe Polisar, the police chief in Albuquerque, NM, who detailed the multi-faceted life of a modern-day law enforcement chief executive.

Downside and Upside

Chief Polisar, a graduate of the FBI National Academy and Harvard University's prestigious program for state and local government executives, pointed out two common downsides of wearing the gold-adorned uniform are the politics and the consistent time drain.

Not surprisingly, politics routinely cropped up as a top misunderstanding many beat officers have of the top cop job they aspire to. "We all answer to civilians ultimately," Polisar told POLICE. "To think otherwise is naïve. Some officers don't understand that."

Chief Bill Liquori, with the Altamonte Springs, FL, Police Department, and a past president of the Florida Police Chiefs Association, stressed that most chiefs operate in a political environment.

Albuquerque's Chief Polisar detailed a rather lengthy list of constituencies all striving to have the ear of their busy chief. Among those groups are neighborhood and business associations, civilians, patrol and superior officers' unions, and special interest groups.

When it comes to officers, Chief Polisar, who worked his way up the ranks and has been with the Albuquerque Police Department since June 1994, said that the chief has to "walk the walk and talk the talk" since "cops are good at seeing through that." The aim is to balance all these seemingly divergent groups, which sometimes involves conflict. All of this takes time.

"No successful chief, whether working in a one- or two-officer agency or in a five- to 10,000-officer department, works a nine-to-five job," said Polisar. "You give up a lot of your personal time, and 14-hour days are not uncommon," he said, adding that discipline is the key which allows him to spend quality time with his wife and two young children.

Chief Sanders called the post a "24-hour-a-day job," echoing the sentiments of Chief Polisar. He said that with beepers, cellular phones and other modern technological advances, "it's just not possible to get away from (the chief's) job."

While off-duty officers may be granted some latitude with their private conduct, chiefs are held to a higher standard. Equally, if not more important than the legal ramifications, the specter of public scrutiny and opinion weighs heavily on the mind of today's chief.

"The chief in the '90's is a figure that represents the department to the public. His or her ethics and private life have to be impeccable, since any off-duty indiscretions can be very damaging to the department," stressed Chief Polisar.

But Polisar countered the negative picture of service as a chief by pointing out, "The good days outweigh the bad days. I get to share in the successes – both big and small – that the department realizes. We've gone from an authorized strength of 770 officers to 928. We've also gotten our officers a 15 percent pay raise over the next two years, and we've experienced a downward crime trend for the first six months of 1997."

Polisar pointed out that most organizations take on the personality of their leader. He said he's proud to have influenced his department, which he dubbed, as expected, "one of the finest law enforcement organizations in the country."

"This is an opportunity to make a difference," said Sanders, who felt that a "high integrity example offered by the chief trickles down to the troops" and permeates the institution.

Competition

Competition to land the top cop slot has become acute. Jobs, whether advertised in the more traditional forums or via word of mouth, generate a large volume of quality applicants.

Russell Arend, director of the well-known Institute of Police Technology and Management (IPTM), said he believed that many of the chief jobs become known via word of mouth.

"It could be that a city is looking for someone who is familiar with computerization or accreditation, and word goes forth in those circles. City managers often call us and ask who we would recommend for their particular need," said Arend speaking from his office in Jacksonville, FL.

Arend added that some states have detailed regulations, such as New Jersey and Pennsylvania, which makes it hard to get in, whereas some other states (such as Connecticut, Florida, Missouri, and Texas, for example) have many outsider chiefs coming aboard.

William Kirchoff, former city manager of Redondo Beach, CA, opined that California, Colorado and Florida become the new homes of law enforcement executives who come from other states. "These three states have non-civil service chief jobs, so the turnover is high," said the author of the book "How Bright is Your Badge: Ways to Successfully Compete for the Best Chief Jobs."

"The pay has improved and there is more freedom of movement," Sanders told POLICE, citing increased compensation as a factor that has added to the glut. "We've actually gotten more of what I call 'gypsy chiefs' who move frequently from department to department, although we still have people who want to stay in-house."

The Washington, DC-based International City Managers' Association (ICMA)'s Public Information Officer, Michele Frisby, said that his organization conducts a compensation survey of their member cities each year. Salaries for chiefs in larger cities are, not surprisingly, higher than those in smaller communities. Resort areas also reflected higher salaries than municipalities in non-resort locales.

As for the states, the July 1996 ICMA study, titled "Compensation '97: An Annual Report on Local Government Executive Salaries and Fringe Benefits," revealed that California came in with the highest average police chief salary ($84,104). West Virginia rounded out the bottom with an average of $31,674.

The International Association of Chiefs of Police's Manager of the Center for Testing Services and Executive Search, Kim J. Kohlhepp, said that they have been inundated with around 100 quality applicants for every nationwide chiefs search they have undertaken. He pointed out that the average "Police Chief" magazine, a monthly publication of the IACP, has advertisements for 10 nationwide chief searches.

The IACP office Koelhepp runs does not act as a placement service, but rather acts on behalf of the contracting governmental entities. He did add, however, that they were open to resumes.

"To be a police chief is a lifelong ambition for many, and they come to the interview process well-prepared," cautioned Kohlhepp to those who seek to enter the choppy chief contender waters.

Many job hopefuls haven't interviewed in years, or at least haven't done so outside of their agency. Basic items such as appropriate suits have become overlooked to their detriment.

Said one aspiring chief who wished to remain nameless: "I was not prepared for the process, which was full of politics and rules I did not encounter in the paramilitary environment of a lower level supervisor."

Selection Process

Reflective of the many different types of law enforcement agencies in the United States, so too are the differing approaches governmental entities take for selecting their most visible representative.

Kohlhepp and Chief Polisar, who himself recently sat on the assessment panel for the El Paso, TX, police chief search, said that the process may range from an informal interview with the mayor, to a formal interview with a selection committee, to a civil service selection system, to the higher level of multiple day assessment centers.

Altamonte Spring's Chief Liquori, a trained assessor, said 200 to 300 applicants are not uncommon. He said that St. Cloud, FL, had 300 applicants. The number was eventually reduced to 10 candidates, who went on to the oral board.

Chief Liquori offered the example of yet another approach that was taken in the Kissimee, FL, chief search that he was also involved in as an assessor: "Kissimee had a reception and all the employees were there partaking in the refreshments. The assessors were there also, seeing how the chief candidates socialized and mingled with the rank and file, consisting of sworn and non-sworn personnel."

Kirchoff said that any lifelong ambition requires planning, and the chief quest is no different.

Experience

"The key is to be a well-rounded, experienced officer," said "Your Badge..." author Kirchoff, who has interviewed and hired many chiefs in his career. "Get experience in patrol, since that is the guts of the operation, but also work in administration."

Chief Sanders underscored the importance of experience. "A serious candidate should come forward with a resume that reflects a knowledgeable base of his department's operations. He should work in investigations, staff services, supply and so forth to develop an understanding of all areas of the department and how they fit together."

The IACP president, who is an 18-year veteran with a master's degree in public administration, said that "uniformed personnel think the detectives have it made and vice versa." He said the exposure of many assignments helps to put that erroneous theory to rest along with many others.

Many of the hiring honchos look for a substantial track record of five to 10 years of managerial experience in several areas of an agency. The goal is to create a well-rounded executive.

Education and Training

All interviewed stressed the importance of an education. "Bachelor's degree minimum, master's degree preferred," was the phrase universally espoused. Chief Liquori and Kirchoff stated that a lot of chiefs now hold doctorates and law degrees.

"Every job has many applicants. Formal education and training make for better police chiefs, and are the ticket for admission to the job," said Chief Sanders.

Professional schools, such as the FBI National Academy and the FBI National Executive Institute, have become a virtual must for those who expect to be in the running for a chief's job in the present era.

Northwestern University's Traffic Institute, based out of Evanston, IL, offers a 350-hour School of Police Staff and Command, which has graduated over 2,500 law enforcement professionals. Held over 10 weeks and offering a variety of scheduling options, the training is geared to prepare law enforcers for senior-level positions.

The IACP, headquartered in Alexandria, VA, has 20 courses under its Leadership/Management Training Program's umbrella, which spans from one to three days in duration. Held at various locales throughout the nation, it concentrates on giving executives the tools to be successful law enforcement managers.

Included in the IACP's offerings is a two-day program titled "How to Become a Police Chief." It is designed for supervisors and mid-level administrators who are considering applying for a police chief's job. Tuition for IACP members is tagged at $300, with non-members doling out $400.

Some jurisdictions require advanced executive or managerial-level certifications from their respective state's P.O.S.T. or training standards entity. According to Bureau Chief Robert Fuller, California's P.O.S.T. (Peace Officer Standards and Training) for example, has enjoyed much success with its Center for Leadership Development, which provides chief-level training on an annual basis.

Research

According to former city manager Kirchoff, one of the biggest mistakes made when attempting to land a particular chief's job is a lack of situation specific knowledge.

"Talk to others who know the city. Go a day early before the interview and go to the local library to read newspapers and find out why the old chief quit. Read the budget and the policies and procedures manual. Find out who you are going to be interviewed by and research them as well," he advised.

The IACP's Kohlhepp concurred: "Almost without exception, the top candidates have done an extensive amount of research. Every resume says 'experience in community relations.' Your accomplishments have to relate to the prospective agency, and thorough research will demonstrate the relevance of your solutions to the agency's problems.

Chief Sanders said that lack of research becomes apparent when the interviewee "tries to become a square peg in a round hole. They're not true to themselves as they're not doing research in the area they applied for."

The competition is stiff and the roadblocks are enormous for those on the quest for the chief's badge. The officers who have planned, studied, worked, and prepared themselves to the highest degree have beaten the odds and successfully made the transition to police chief. These few high-profile men and (increasingly) women seem, by and large, to be pleased with the challenges that come their way on a daily basis.

"It might sound corny," said Albuquerque's Chief Polisar, deeply ensconced in his chief's chair. "To be afforded the opportunity to be chief of police is the honor of a lifetime."

March 2000
Law and Order:
The Magazine for Police Management

Shifting Motivations: Community Service Gives Ground to Aspiring Careerists

Raymond Zamora had a dream. He envisioned himself in the blue uniform of a law enforcement officer and used his service as a sworn volunteer law enforcer as his ticket into the ranks of paid professional policing.

While community service is still among the factors that motivate people to serve as volunteer reserve or auxiliary officers, a shift in the balance between "professional reserves" and full-time officer hopefuls has occurred in the past few years.

In some states (such as California where reserves have to meet the same training criteria as full-timers), the cadre of recently recruited volunteers is almost exclusively made up of younger folks exploring a possible career in policing.

"It's changed over the past few years," said Frank Rizzo, a reserve lieutenant with the Paramus Police Department in Bergen County, NJ. "There has been an increase of people applying to the reserves here in Paramus who are interested in a job as a police officer."

Rizzo estimated that as many as 80 percent of those who apply to join his 18 volunteer officer group are striving to have a police paycheck in their future.

"There is less of an emphasis on community service in society and more on a career and being recognized by the department or another local agency to help the person get a police job," said Rizzo, who works full-time as the president of a Jersey City, NJ, printing company.

Increased familial and work pressures also combine to push more professional reservists away. The increasingly rare breed of people who serve year after year out of personal interest now have trouble justifying the time commitment involved in being a reserve officer.

Like an education or vocational training, volunteer service as a reserve officer has become for many justifiable as a conduit to a career choice. While some lament the shift in motivating factors, others see the move as positive for law enforcement and the public they serve.

"Initially, I wanted to know that I could do it (law enforcement). It was insecurity within myself," said Zamora, who now patrols as a salaried deputy sheriff in Santa Fe County, NM. "From the outside looking in, I did not know whether I could do it."

Zamora served over six years with the New Mexico Department of Corrections in the infamous Penitentiary at Santa Fe. He certainly knew he had the mettle to deal with criminal elements in the familiar surroundings of the incarceration facility. But fielding calls in the vast unknown of the state capital county's law enforcement jurisdiction was a challenge.

"I wanted to be a full-time deputy, and working as a reserve deputy helped me to be sure so I could change jobs," he said. It was that impetus which first drove him to don the uniform and gun as a reserve deputy sheriff and later as a full-timer.

Firsthand Experience

With television and movies pumping out distorted images of law enforcement personnel and the work they undertake every day, aspiring law enforcers are subject to erroneous impressions as well. Service as a reserve officer is one way for them to get a realistic view of the job.

"It's a great training ground. You have to start somewhere and being a reserve officer really tells you what you are getting into," said Rizzo, a certified field training officer.

The down side for Rizzo is that he only rides with new reserves. He said he misses the benefits of riding with other experienced officers.

Rizzo said that most of their new reservists leave after two to three years for a paid officer slot. Paramus' reserve force is in a continual rookie officer training mode, which detracts from other aspects of the volunteer officer stint.

On the plus side, from the department's perspective, the reserve stint gives prospective employers a track record of performance prior to the expense of full-time hiring. In this age of liability concerns agencies that hire reserves have a small window of police service that can be checked for potential problems before a large taxpayer disbursement.

"We knew pretty much what we had with Raymond before he was hired on full-time," Stacy S. Saiz said of the decision to add Zamora to the payroll. Saiz served as Zamora's supervisor when he was a reserve and later when he changed status. The former patrol sergeant, who now works for the New Mexico Law Enforcement Academy in Santa Fe, said the familiarity was an advantage for both Zamora and the Sheriff's Department.

As a reserve deputy, Zamora was uniformed, armed, and deployed the same as a full-time deputy on patrol in the 2,500 square mile jurisdiction. He got a real taste of his future paycheck and the department was able to ensure that they hired a full-timer with a track record of hard work, a sharp appearance and good community interaction skills. Rizzo agreed that hiring agencies have a better sense of the police applicant's abilities and qualities when that person has served as a volunteer in uniform. His reserves get their fair share of activity as they assist the 94 full-time officer agency in patrolling a 28,000 population, 40-square mile municipality located 20 minutes west of New York City.

But the ticket for entry as a reserve officer has become harder to come by- due in part to the rising use of reserve organizations in many agencies as a pre-screening tool for those in search of a salaried position.

"More people in our applicant pool want the job of a regular police officer today. We as reserve program administrators have to be more stringent before letting them in," Rizzo said.

As with many of the changes that occur in policing, law enforcement executives and officers alike are adapting to the challenge and finding advantages manifested in the transformations.

"If it weren't for my time serving as a reserve, I probably wouldn't have become a full-time deputy," Zamora said. "As a reserve, everyone, including me, got a look at my performance and my feelings for the job. That is why I do this every day and love working in law enforcement."

October 19, 2005
Officer.com

The Good, the Bad, and the Ugly of Online College Degrees

Whether in New Mexico, North Carolina, or Florida, you can hear the same concerns aired by veteran police officers and deputy sheriffs nationwide; they need college education to compete for promotions, but their rotating schedules slow down their eagerness to get back into a traditional college environment. Heavily marketed online college degrees seem to be the answer to many, but it is not a path to be taken without some knowledge of the online education industry.

Care needs to be taken to avoid money at a degree that may be viewed as the product of a diploma mill. Online colleges that promise "credit for life's experience" with little academic work or rigor are probably too good to be true and may backfire on you later.

Accreditation

Many online colleges advertise themselves as accredited. It is important to dig through their website and find out who their accrediting organization is. The next move is to go to that accrediting body's website and confirm through a search that the accrediting organization is legitimate. There are six regional accrediting entities that are recognized by established educational institutions. This is important if you are seeking to go on for a higher degree and want the lower degree acknowledged or if your employer will view a non-accredited degree as "resume fraud."

The six regional accreditation bodies are: the Middle States Association of Colleges and Schools (Delaware, District of Columbia, Maryland, New Jersey, New York, Pennsylvania, Puerto Rico), the New England Association of Schools and Colleges (Connecticut, Maine, Massachusetts, New Hampshire, Rhode Island, and Vermont), the North Central Association of Colleges and Schools (Arkansas, Arizona, Colorado, Iowa, Illinois, Indiana, Kansas, Michigan, Minnesota, Missouri, North Dakota, Nebraska, Ohio, Oklahoma, New Mexico, South Dakota, Wisconsin, West Virginia, and Wyoming), the Northwest Association of Schools and Colleges (Alaska, Idaho, Utah, Montana, Nevada, Oregon, and Washington), the Southern Association of Colleges and Schools (Alabama, Florida, Georgia, Kentucky, Louisiana, Mississippi, North Carolina, South Carolina, Tennessee, Texas, and Virginia), and the Western Association of Schools and Colleges.

Many online institutions throw out the term "accredited" without any further explanation. Some have gone so far as to make up their own accrediting bodies with legitimate sounding names. Beware of those and don't waste your money.

National accrediting bodies, such as the Distance Education Training Council (DETC), have cropped up and have become a little more accepted. DETC and their type are not, however, accepted at all other institutions and employers.

Some religious based online colleges have religious accreditations, but do not have one of the six regional accreditation groups' stamp of approval. Again, depending what you are trying to do with the degree, you may or may not have a religious accreditation accepted.

Private Colleges

Large private corporations, with their attention to student service, have taken a chunk of business from the traditional colleges and have been growing at a healthy pace. Some of the larger names in the field (that are regionally accredited) include the University of Phoenix, Northcentral University, Kaplan College, ITT Tech, Walden University, and Capella University. Newer entrants that have established a foothold with criminal justice students are the University of Cincinnati and Boston University.

Private corporations, such as the Apollo Group behind the huge University of Phoenix operation, really jumpstarted the distance learning field a few years ago and nudged the traditional "bricks and mortar" institutions to jump into the fray. They are often viewed by their traditionally rooted colleagues as being less academically rigorous. Prospective students sometimes report that they are pressured to enroll and feel that profit is the main motivator.

Public Universities

Feeling the pressure from the privateers, respectable public universities (commonly referred to as "bricks and mortars") have jumped into the distance learning pond. Longtime players such as Florida State University, University of Wisconsin at Platteville, and Michigan State University have established degrees up to the master's level. East Carolina University has also established reputable programs.

The public universities tend to have greater prestige within academic circles, but they often lag in customer service and have greater admissions hoops to jump through than the private online programs. For example, public universities tend to require that the successful applicant to their program attain a certain score on standardized tests such as the Graduate Record Exam (GRE) for entrance to master's degree study. High school grade point averages can take a more significant role in this route.

Choosing a Major

Beyond a personal intellectual curiosity, determining what you want to do with the degree is a first step to deciding what major you want to take. Officers have increasingly branched beyond criminal justice or criminology degrees to take on majors in areas such as political science, sociology, psychology, business, and public administration. Newer fields, such as homeland security, have also been developed.

If you are looking at teaching criminal justice associate's degree students in a community college setting, you will need a master's degree in criminal justice or a master's degree in another field with 18 additional credit hours in criminal justice. Employing colleges will look at the prospective instructor's official transcripts to see course prefixes such as CRJ or CRIM.

Other officers settle on criminal justice as a major after they examine their agency's tuition reimbursement or promotion policies to find that only courses in criminal justice qualify for recognition. Still other departments may only grant educational pay incentives if the degree was in criminal justice. It is wise to check your agency's policy beforehand.

Some officers are aspiring to become a police chief or city manager. Their future office requires a broader set of skills that are more appropriately developed with a major in public administration, public affairs, business administration, or management.

If a second career in the private sector appears attractive, computer programming or networking may be the route to take. Business administration could also work for you.

Many officers find themselves becoming skilled crisis interventionists through their job and look to counseling as an area to develop on the side or after retirement. Psychology or counseling becomes an attractive route.

The exposure to the legal system make some officers look towards law school. While there are no American Bar Association accredited online law schools yet, there are a few that are recognized for those that want to take the California bar exam. Good undergraduate majors to prepare for law school include English and political science which develop thinking and written communication skills.

Residency Requirements

Some of the distance learning colleges are fully online while others require some time on campus. It could be one weekend or week per year. The on campus time requirement is more prevalent at the graduate (master's and doctorate) level than at the associate's and bachelor's degree level.

The on campus requirement may not be practical for all students and the presence of this mandate should be investigated prior to committing your time and financial resources.

Costs

Online education can be pricey especially with the large, national for profit entities. Nationally accredited Kaplan has 90 credit associate's degree and 180 credit bachelor's degrees programs at $280 a credit hour. The 55 credit hour master's degree in criminal justice comes in at $350 per credit hour.

Even the public educational institutions can be pricey. For example, the regionally accredited University of Wisconsin at Platteville's 30 credit hour criminal justice master's degree program comes in at $550 per credit.

A factor to consider that few programs point out is additional cost in books and materials. One regionally accredited online college, Touro University International, has taken a novel approach and included materials in the cost of the course ($1,000 per bachelor's degree course).

Research

Before plunging into an online program, it pays to do your research. Any information source should be judged for its credibility and independence from any online educational institution. An excellent source for further information is DegreeInfo.com (especially the forums section). John Bear is a leading authority who has written extensively on the distance learning topic.

Before commencing on the distance learning route, it pays to study the options. Only the educated prospective student will make the proper choices that will benefit your career in the long run.

January 12, 2006
Officer.com

Inside the FBI National Academy: The FBI NA and others are key to promotion

Here's what we think of your ##@@**!! Yellow brick!" said the note on top of the shoebox on top of the New Jersey police chief's desk. He had returned to his office only to find his coveted gold painted brick, which was awarded to him when he completed the famed yellow brick road long distance run at the end of his stint at the prestigious FBI National Academy, was smashed into pieces. While the pulverized brick turned out to be fake, substituted as part of a practical joke by officers in his agency, the pride he felt from having attended the FBI National Academy was certainly real.

Long thought of as one of the final rungs in the career development training ladder for aspiring police chiefs, the FBI National Academy in Quantico, VA is geared to executive level law enforcement officers. The eleven-week school, and a few others, should be on your radar as you map out your long-term training goals.

Many qualified police executive training schools are out there. They vary as to duration, academic rigor, reputation, and cost. This "Career Corner" column offers some information for you to consider regarding several top tier command officer training schools.

FBI National Academy

The grand-daddy of schools, the FBI National Academy has been around since July 5, 1935. It is a ten-week program whose major benefit to graduates is the ability to network with police power brokers from all of the nation and internationally. Graduates of the FBI National Academy are able to join the 15,000 plus member FBI National Academy Associates. Many see the networking aspect as the largest benefit of attendance.

Each session finds the attendees living at the dorms of the Quantico facility and taking a track of academic and physical learning that earns them undergraduate credit hours from the University of Virginia. Depending on the attendees' academic background, the stint could seem difficult or easy. Three papers or so are done by most with the length ranging from eight to ten pages for each. The physical aspect can be capped by the optional, but respected, yellow brick run long distance course.

For some, the ultimate substantive value of the FBI National Academy is in question. One police chief stated that when he arrived, he found the curriculum very light and was told to "perpetuate the myth." Others have lamented that the "college dorm" mentality was present with grown men away from home pulling stunts such as stealing the academy flag and short-sheeting each other's' beds.

However, there is no doubt that the over 38,000 students, including 2,835 international officers, thought enough of the establishment to attend one of the 220 sessions that have been held. Another plus, especially from the perspective of budget conscious managers, is the cost free aspect with the feds picking up the tab.

Southern Police Institute

Like the FBI, the Southern Police Institute has a number of offerings with their executive school being the top of their heap. The Administrative Officers Course is their 12 week version of police executive development. Two sessions are held each year since the entity was established in 1951.

Attending officers can earn 15 undergraduate credit hours in five garnered from SPI's parent, the University of Louisville's Department of Justice Administration. Those individuals with a bachelor's degree already are eligible to pursue nine graduate credit hours.

Students are housed at the Belknap Campus of the University of Louisville in Louisville, KY. Again, students are away for an extended time and have opportunities to network with officers from other agencies. They are able to do so via the Southern Police Institute's Alumni Association.

Northwestern University

With around 800 graduates, Northwestern University's School of Police Staff and Command has been a popular option for many police administrators due to its travelling location convenience. In addition to its ten week course held at its main Evanston, IL, location, the 45 officer maximum enrollment classes are hosted by agencies around the country. Host agencies can even get free seats by filling up the seats with paying students from other agencies.

Northwestern University goes even further and allows for creative scheduling such as breaking the course attendance over a longer time frame with short stints making up each component. That appeals to many bosses not willing to part with their employees for an extended time frame.

Police Executive Research Forum

A much shorter stint in duration, the Washington, DC-based Police Executive Research Forum's Senior Management Institute for Police is held at Boston University. With the exception of weekends, senior police managers stay in the college's residence facility in Boston, MA, and participate in a case study approach to law enforcement and public policy issues.

Be warned because the course is fairly intensive given the nature of its brief schedule. There are reading assignments beforehand and successful completion requires the ability to complete research papers.

Considerations

When you examine these courses and others like them to determine which one you should attend, you'll need to examine a host of evaluative criteria. Most officers do not get the option of going to all of the schools out there, so you want to be sure that the one you pick fits the cost, learning aims, time commitment, career, family, and political considerations that you have set for yourself.

A key item to consider is can you afford to be away from your agency. There are political ramifications for many senior level police executives if they are absent for any extended period of time.

A long time away from your agency may set you up for an organizational coup by the person or persons who have stepped into your shows during your absence. Many political problems can crop up, so the establishment of solid base of support is crucial to your jetting off. Your key constituencies need to buy into the value of you and your leaning to ensure your career stability.

Along the same lines, a key constituency often overlooked is family. A long time away for a father or mother with a troubled teenager in the household may not be appropriate. In that case, a more flexible, locally hosted program, such as that offered by Northwestern University, may be ideal for you.

Cost is also a factor. Northwestern University's School of Police Staff and Command can cost in the area of $3,000 for the course. At the other end of the spectrum, the FBI picks up the cost for those attending the FBI National Academy. In any event, your employer is still paying your salary while you are away soaking in the knowledge and they may not be so keen on the expenditure. A few people, including yours truly, have even ended up paying their own way to advanced training as a condition for their employer allowing them to go.

The learning experience, like in a college setting, is rally predicated on what you make of it. Some people just skirt by, while others pour their heart and soul into the endeavor. You'll need to identify which category you belong in. If you were in the not so academically inclined category, an intense program such as that offered by PERF would not be a comfortable fit for you.

A good strategy is to identify people who are serving in positions that you have aspirations of taking on some day. Find out from them (or their agency's website online biography) what executive training program they attended. Find out if that program is well regarded by your bosses and key constituencies.

With a bit of research, you should be able to identify the law enforcement executive training school that is right for you. The faculty at the schools may facilitate the knowledge being available to you, but it is up to you to make the right learning opportunity happen.

July 2, 2007
PoliceLink.com

So you wanna be a cop… first impressions count

When PoliceLink.com asked me to write a new column, I looked at it as a golden opportunity to get the word out to aspiring law enforcement officers on how to achieve the goal of pinning on that silver badge. In m y former role as a police chief and current job overseeing police academies in Florida, I am well-acquainted with the mistakes and issues that shoot people down in their bid to be a police officer, deputy sheriff, state trooper, or other law enforcer type. This column is designed to help you avoid those pitfalls.

The first step is to determine whether you have to be hired by a law enforcement agency and then attend the basic law enforcement academy or if you have to the option of paying your way through an academy in order to make yourself more attractive for hire after graduation. In keeping with the home rule policing concept in our democratic society, each area of the country goes about the process in its own distinctive style.

In either case, you're probably going to have to go by the academy or department at some point to pick up material such as the application packet. You've heard about the job openings from such places as PoliceLink.com, a department's website recruiting page, or newspaper advertisement. You need to make the first step and pick up the application package.

Here are five things to bear in mind that could make or break you early on in the process. They will also help you later in the process.

1. Dress for success. While future columns will delve into more detail on this topic, the old phrase dress for success rings true. Do not, as I have seen countless hopefuls do, show up wearing baggy pants or gold jewelry hanging out everywhere. And don't forget the personal hygiene. You want to show that you are capable of presenting yourself as a professional at all times, not just in a formal oral board or interview. I would hear the negative comments that front desk staff said referring to aspiring coppers who walked in from a night out club hopping. Dress in a suitable business attire. Make a good impression on all the people you come into contact with entering the building; not just those with gold badges.

2. Check out your car and your driving. Make sure you drive sensibly. Of course, you should always drive responsibly. Screeching your car's tires in the police parking lot does not help to convince nearby officers of your ability to one day drive their patrol unit safely. As an administrator, I even sent officers to the parking lot to check out the aspiring recruit's vehicle. Believe me they will certainly waste no opportunity to voice their concerns. You should also make sure that your car is clean, neat and up-to-date on registration, inspection, tires, etc. That's all a part of appearing presentable and being law-abiding.

3. Arrive early. If you have an appointment to pick up the materials, make sure you arrive early. Many receptionists note your time in the door and pass that information on to the boss. If you arrive late when it is assumed that you are trying to make a good impression, it doesn't leave much hope for when you've landed the cop job.

4. Be respectful. This should go without saying. Get used to being polite and using phrases such as yes, sir and yes, ma'am. It may sound old-fashioned, but it goes a long way within the police world and even with the public. Be respectful with all people that you encounter, especially secretaries. While often overlooked by the officer applicants, they are the ones who really have the ear of the brass and can build you up or tear you down in later conversations behind closed doors.

5. Have a plan of action. Before you leave the building with application materials in hand, diplomatically find out from the front office staff or other representative what the steps are in the process and what you have to do next. Request a business card and take notes if you have to, but chances are that the steps are all outlined in the printed recruitment package. Figure out the timetable for those steps and keep on top of the deadlines.

These five steps are but the very first rungs in your police job ladder. Now you have the materials in hand and can eagerly read through them when sit down in your car. By following this column's advice, you should keep yourself from being knocked out of the process in the early stages.

October 30, 2007
PoliceLink.com

Promotions: The Courses That Count

You've decided to go back to college. You figured how to pay for it (or have your agency do so). You've set up a place in your home to study for exams and do papers. But here's the question that many people ask…what should you study? Picking a major has never been harder than it is now. With the explosion of online and private institutions of higher education, aspiring and current law enforcers have more choices than ever. That includes the many choices of majors or areas of study.

College in this day and age of complicated policing in a democratic society makes for a good move. In the words of my good friend and retired South Brunswick, NJ, Police chief Fred Thompson, "Education does not make a bad cop good, but it makes a good cop better." Similarly, the choice of a major does not make a bad cop good, but the right major can position you to do your job even better or get your foot in the door at your dream department.

The key is determining what your goal is with that educational endeavor. Is the goal promotion or is it the furtherance of an area that is integrated into policing such as counseling? Do you want to be the man (or woman) in the corner suite, or are you looking to be the best patrol officer you can be?

Promotion Path

Many students view education as just a piece of paper that is their ticket to the gold on the collar. But an education is more than that. A good education (stress good as in quality) will enhance an officer's skills and talents. Better written and verbal communications skills are but two of many benefits derived from an education.

But of course, an education, particularly an advanced graduate education doesn't hurt your chances of promotion (in most places). Many agencies have established minimum educational credentials for promotion. The higher up the food chain, the more letters (college degrees) will probably need to follow your name.

Those looking toward the executive suite would be smart to major in an area that shows police command staff that you possess the tools to do a managerial post. Aspirations to the police chief post require this even more as proof to the hiring city manager that the candidate has the skills to do the complex job.

Degrees (especially a master's degree) in business administration, public administration, or public affairs are especially suited for those envisioning a career path that moves up in the organization. My master's degree is in public administration with a specialization in criminal justice. That served me well in my successful application for a police chief's post as the hiring city manager had a master's degree in public administration also.

Allied Area

If you are looking to expand or enhance your credentials in an area allied with law enforcement, the right major can help you make that happen. I know officers that demonstrated a knack for talking to people in their role as cops and wanted to pursue that on a higher level. They attained degrees in social work, counseling, and psychology. Some have even opened up part-time counseling practices and are honing their craft.

A newer area for officers is forensic cyber-crime and computers. A few years back, only a handful of agencies had anyone who understood computers, let alone had the requisite knowledge to spearhead a computer based crime investigation. Nowadays, however, more and more law enforcers are earning computer-based degree credentials and are comfortable dealing in the cyber world.

With the growing diversification of the communities that are served by law enforcement agencies, officers responding to calls for police services are seeing a huge increase in the number of languages and divergent cultures. Degrees that offer immersion in foreign languages and their cultures are attractive as they offer officers a path to meet that modern policing challenge.

Certain rare languages may have more cache than others given a particular agency's needs. For example, some agencies in the Central Florida region are very interested in those who speak Creole. Others, especially in the intelligence areas, are very interested in those people who can communicate in Arabic languages from the Middle East. Still others, such as those in the Pacific Northwest, are pursuing people who can speak Korean and other Pacific Rim languages.

With the rise of white-collar crime, some law enforcement organizations are very interested in those who have a credentialed forensic accounting background. Like cyber-crime expertise, accounting is not a common degree that police recruiters and administrators encounter.

Whatever your choice, the most important thing is just to do it. The bosses at headquarters will recognize you as a person who has chosen a task and stuck with it to completion. They will have more confidence that you will take on new or additional responsibilities in the same manner.

April 2008
PoliceLink.com

Getting Serious About Joining the Force

It's a New Year and you want to fulfill your dream of landing that cop job. Now that the initial flurry of silly New Year's Resolutions have fallen by the wayside, let's get serious. In order to help you on that quest, this Cop Career Counselor column is geared towards helping you shape your New Year's resolutions towards that goal.

Around 80% of Police Departments and Sheriff's Offices across the country are experiencing a crisis in recruiting. Some departments have altered their standards in response. The Dallas Police Department just revamped their prior drug usage history for applicants (A one-time, experimental usage of a harder drug such as cocaine is now okay with a ten year or older window).

Be that as it may, the standards are still high in most agencies. Only the most determined of applicants will make it in. The time to alter habits is today (if not years ago). Here are some useful New Year's Resolutions to replace the initial silly ones.

Have a fitness program- This is an age-old New Year's resolution. Health club memberships skyrocket this time of year reflective of many people's desire to better their physique. Be wise. Do your research and start the program under the guidance of medical and fitness professionals.

Toss the Tobacco- Some agencies have enacted tobacco-free policies. As cities in particular have been squeezed by soaring health insurance costs, administrators see the requirement of police applicants to have been tobacco free for a year as a move towards lowered costs.

Clean up the Credit- Do as the financial gurus advise and take stock of your money situation. If you have outstanding bills, contact those creditors and set up a payment plan. Put those high interest credit cards at the top of your list.

Slow Down on the Driving- Police chiefs and sheriffs recognize the high liability they have from their law enforcers driving 6,000 pound weapons. A ticket-laden pre-hire driving record will make any on-duty crash situations into a negligent hiring lawsuit against the employing agency. Try to put some distance between your application and your tickets.

Get New Friends- Don't be the guy who gets caught on surveillance cameras bailing out bad guys from the county jail. Prospective law enforcers are judged in part by their choice in friends and associates.

Quit Clubbin'- Hanging out at downtown clubs and other places of adult distractions are not conducive to a healthy police career. You don't want to be the person who ends up being in the wrong place at the wrong time and gets caught in the net. Your explanations as to why you are on the police report will be lost to a background investigator who is wondering why you were in such a place to begin with.

Bag the Baggy Pants- In order to be perceived positively as a future professional law enforcer, you need to dress the part all the time. Putting on the suit and tie when you go to the oral board is not enough. Donning baggy pants for your stroll in the mall will not go over well when you run into the local captain or major doing some shopping with the family. Present yourself professionally at all times as you do not know who will bump into around town.

The time to live the clean police lifestyle is not when you pin on the badge. The answer is actually to the contrary. The time to conduct yourself at the higher standard is now (and really yesterday). Much like the motto "dress for success," you have "behave better for success" as a police applicant.

July 2008
PoliceLink.com

Sample Police Exam Questions

1) Instructions: Read the notes from a call for police service. Pick the answer that most correctly represents the information.

Notes: Responded to domestic at 100 Main Street. Spoke with victim Jane Jones. Observed visible injury laceration on Jane Jones' right forearm. Jones refused to cooperate.

a. I responded to a domestic. Upon my arrival, I spoke with the victim, Jane Jones. I observed a visible injury laceration on her right forearm. Ms. Jones refused to cooperate with my investigation.

b. I responded to 100 Main Street in reference to a domestic. Upon my arrival, I spoke with the victim, Jane Jones. I observed a visible injury laceration on her right forearm. Ms. Jones refused to cooperate with my investigation.

c. I spoke with the victim, Jane Jones. I observed a visible injury laceration on her right forearm. Ms. Jones refused to cooperate with my investigation.

d. I responded to a domestic. Upon my arrival, I spoke with the victim, Jane Jones. I observed a visible injury laceration on her right forearm.

Correct answer: B

2) Instructions: Read the notes from a call for police service. Pick the answer that most correctly represents the information.

Notes: Flagged down at 1st Street and Avenue A by complainant/victim John Smith. Smith robbed at gunpoint approx. 10:00 am. Unknown suspect WM, 5'7", 150 lbs., clean-shaven, slim, black t-shirt, jeans. Took $10.00 bill headed West on 1st Street.

a. I was flagged down at 1st and Avenue A by complainant/victim John Smith. Mr. Smith told me that approx. 20 minutes previously, at 10:00 am, he was robbed at gunpoint of a ten dollar bill at the same location. Mr. Smith described the suspect as a white male, around 5'7" in height, 150 pounds, clean-shaven with a slim build. He further described him as wearing a black t-shirt and jeans. Mr. Smith saw him leaving the area on foot headed west on 1st Street.

b. John Smith told me that approx. 20 minutes previously, at 10:00 am, he was robbed at gunpoint of a ten dollar bill at the same location. Mr. Smith described the suspect as a white male, around 5'7" in height, 150 pounds, clean-shaven with a slim build. He further described him as wearing a black t-shirt and jeans. Mr. Smith saw him leaving the area on foot headed west on 1st Street.

c. John Smith described the suspect as a white male, around 5'7" in height, 150 pounds, clean-shaven with a slim build. He further described him as wearing a black t-shirt and jeans. Mr. Smith saw him leaving the area on foot headed west on 1st Street. John Smith told me that approx. 20 minutes previously, at 10:00 am, he was robbed at gunpoint of a ten dollar bill at the same location.

d. John Smith was robbed. Male suspect fled west on 1st Street.

Answer: A

3) Read the following paragraph. Then look away from the paragraph (you are on your honor) and choose the correct answer.

Officer Cosgriff responded to a residential burglary. The victim stated that, while he was on vacation between 7/2/08 at 4:00 pm and 7/8/08 at 11:00 am, person or persons unknown did unlawfully enter his residence and take his property.

When did the victim discover the burglary to his residence?

a. 7/2/08 at 4:00 pm
b. 7/2/08 at 11:00 am
c. 7/8/08 at 4:00 pm
d. 7/8/08 at 11:00 am

Answer: D

4) Read the following paragraph. Then look away from the paragraph (you are on your honor) and choose the correct answer.

Deputy Weinblatt responded to an armed robbery in progress. Upon his arrival, he was advised that the suspect fled in a late model blue Honda Accord sedan.

The vehicle was described as a

a. 2008 blue Honda Accord
b. late model dark blue Honda Accord
c. late model blue Honda Accord sedan
d. late model blue Honda Accord

Answer: C

5) Referring to the last scenario, Deputy Weinblatt responded to:

a. A robbery in progress
b. An armed robbery in progress
c. A burglary in progress

d. An armed robbery that happened in the past

Answer: B

6) Read the following paragraph. Then look away from the paragraph (you are on your honor) and choose the correct answer.

Gang Unit Investigator Cosgriff fills out a field interview (FI) card on a suspected gang member. The gang member's street name is "Killer G" and he is a documented member of the Eastside Boys. "Killer G" has numerous tattoos that help to verify his gang status including a tear tattoo on his face, an "EB" tattoo on his left chest over his heart, and a tattoo of a compass with a large "E" on his right forearm.

"Killer G" has how many tattoos?

a. 1
b. 2
c. 3
d. 4

Answer: C

7) Referring to the last scenario, "Killer G" had an "EB" tattoo on his

a. right forearm
b. right chest
c. face
d. left chest

Answer: D

8) Departmental policy requires that all officers that use force must complete a written use of force report. The report must include the circumstances leading up the officer's decision to use force, the level of force used, the justification for the force used, and the outcome of the officer's use of force.

The departmental policy requires:

a. That officers explain to suspects why they are using force before such force is utilized
b. That officers explain verbally why the circumstances leading up the officer's decision to use force, the level of force used, the justification for the force used, and the outcome of the officer's use of force.
c. That officers explain in a use of force report the circumstances leading up the officer's decision to use force, the level of force used, the justification for the force used, and the outcome of the officer's use of force.
d. That no use of force report be filled out if no injury resulted from said use of force.

Answer: C

9) You are a city police officer on patrol and observe a car driving left of center and not stopping for a stop sign. You stop the car and, upon speaking with the driver, you believe that the driver is DUI. You also

note that the driver is a member of your employing municipality's city council. You should:

a. Give the city council member a ride home.
b. Allow the city council member to go on his way in his car.
c. Continue as you would normally with your investigation and notify your supervisor.
d. Write a citation for the two traffic violations and release the driver.

Answer: C

10) You are on patrol with your Field Training Officer (FTO) and respond to a commercial burglar alarm at a grocery store. Upon responding, you and your FTO find an open door with no sign of forced entry. After successfully clearing the store, your FTO grabs a case of water and says no one will miss it. You should:

a. Ask for your share of the water
b. Tell him to put the water back
c. Ignore the situation since you are new to the department
d. Report the situation to your FTO's supervisor.

Answer: D

11) Your department has a written policy that forbids officers from taking any bribes, gratuities, or gifts. You stop at a local diner and find that the waitress wants to give you the police officer 50% discount. You should:

a. Leave money on the table equal to the full amount of what the published menu price and normal tip you would have left.
b. Argue with the waitress and manager insisting on paying the full bill.
c. Walk out not paying anything.
d. Pay the bill as indicated with the 50% discount.

12) Miranda v. Arizona was a very important U.S. Supreme Court case from 1966 that affected law enforcement officers. Among other things, the rape case involving migrant farm worker Ernesto Miranda dictated that a warning must be given to suspects who are not free leave if they are questioned as to specifics of the case.

The paragraph above dictates that:

a. Miranda warnings must be given anytime a suspect is placed in handcuffs
b. Miranda warnings must be given if the suspect is questioned as to the specifics of the crime and he or she is not free to leave.
c. Miranda warnings must be given in rape cases.
d. Miranda warnings must be given to all people interviewed by law enforcement officers.

Answer: B

13) Carroll v. United States was a 1925 U.S. Supreme Court case that clarified a law enforcement exception to the search warrant requirement of the 4th Amendment. Under the Carroll Doctrine, as it is now known, law

enforcement officers may search automobiles without a search warrant as long as they have probable cause to do so and the automobile is movable.

The paragraph above dictates:

a. Officers may only search an automobile with the written voluntary consent of the driver.
b. Officers may search an automobile since the car is movable.
c. Officers may search an automobile without a search warrant as long as they have probable cause to do so and the automobile is movable.
d. Officers may not search an automobile

Answer: C

14) New York v. Belton, a 1981 U.S. Supreme Court case, clarified that law enforcement officers, upon making an arrest, may search any the immediate "lunge area" within the reach of the arrestee including any open or closed containers. Such a search may be conducted at the same time as the arrest.

The paragraph above dictates that:

a. Officers may search the vicinity of the arrestee including any open or closed containers.
b. Officers must have consent to search the area around the arrestee.
c. Officers may search beyond the reach or "lunge area" of the arrestee.

d. Officers may not search any further than the person they have arrested.

Answer: A

15) Which sentence below is grammatically correct?

a. I am an educated person who wants to be a police officer.
b. I am an educated person whom wants to be a police officer.
c. I am an educated people who wanted to be a police officer.
d. I was an educated person who wants to be police officers.

Answer: A

July 2008
PoliceLink.com

10 Tips for Acing the Police Entrance Exam

While police entrance processes vary widely from state to state, and even from department to department, most law enforcement applicant screening processes begin with the written exam. By starting with the written exam, most sheriffs and police chiefs (having been one I understand this concept) use the written exam as just that: a screening tool. Written exams are a fairly cheap way to knock out numerous applicants before they get to the more costly aspects of the process. Such more expensive steps could include background investigations, physicals and psychological exams.

Some agencies use the written exam as a way to move people out of the process. They don't use it as a ranking tool. Other parts of the process (such as the oral review panel) may be where placement on eligibility lists originates.

Other agencies may give you extra points to be applied to your exam score. Among the favored stats groups that may be awarded additional points are: military veterans, already employed state certified law enforcement officers working for another agency, bilingual speakers with language fluency in local demand, and children of law enforcement officers who have died in the line of duty. Whatever the use or interpretation of the entrance exam, one thing is clear: it can stop you from advancing further in the process. Here are ten tips to help you through the exam.

1) Getting Additional Points. As alluded to above, see if any group gets additional points. The agency may have identified a need and tried to encourage the filling of the gap by awarding points. You may be lucky enough to be a member of a group that the agency wants badly.

2) Research the type of test. To know what to study, you need to ascertain what type of test is given by the agency. The PoliceLink.com discussion boards are an excellent source of information. Find out what previous members say about the test. Don't get discouraged by value judgments on the process or bank on a reporting of the actual test questions (that would be unethical). You only want to get a feel for what type of test it is.

You may also be able to check with the testing agency. Many agencies offer or can point you to a study guide. Many of those study guides have sample questions that you can use to gauge your baseline ability to score well.

3) Shore up areas of weakness. Once you have identified the type of test questions being utilized and have done a self-assessment, you need to work to strengthen your perceived areas of vulnerability. For example, some agencies have a math component on their exam. Many people have problems with this section of the exam as it has been years since they have done math problems. The Internet has many sites that you can check out and self-tutor yourself.

4) Eat right. Try to avoid eating heavily or skipping the meal prior to the test. You want to eat light and avoid sugar-laden or heavily processed foods.

5) Mark your answers clearly and erase fully. Clear answer indicators are especially important if the test answer sheet is a Scantron type. With this type of answer sheet, the test taker fills in a little dot (corresponding with an answer letter) using a number two lead pencil. False error readings often result if the Scrantron scanner reader fails to detect an improperly filled in dot. While I don't advocate changing your answer (as indicated above), make sure that you fully erase the pencil mark in the dot if you decide to do so.

6) Don't change answers. After years of administering exams, I have found that the old adage holds true: stick with your first answer. In most cases, when you change the answer, you have changed it to a wrong answer. Your gut reaction is probably right.

7) Get plenty of sleep. Cramming the night before and staying up late has proven to bring back very little

return for the sacrifice. You want your mind to be alert and fully functional. This is especially true if it is a long exam.

8) Don't last minute cram. Having taken a few exams in my career, I am amazed by the people cramming in their car just minutes before taking an exam. Studying is best accomplished in smaller increments over time. I have always felt that creates additional stress. If you don't know it by the time of the test, a few minutes of last minute cramming is not going to help and may even hurt.

9) Read questions carefully. I have observed that many people fail because they neglected to read the questions with due care. This is especially relevant when the test uses terms like "not," "never," and "only."

Look at other questions. If you are unsure of an answer, leave it blank and come back to it later. Other questions may contain the answer that you were contemplating. If you do this, be sure to comply with the advice in number ten below.

10) Proof read test. Before you turn in your test answer sheet, be sure to check it over. Test takers often leave answers blank and that impacts their final score. This also gives you a chance to go back and answer those hard to figure out answers.

The bottom line in taking law enforcement entrance exams is to take the care in preparation and execution that employers want to see in the actual performance of police service duties.   With attention to detail, most people should score well and leap over the first of many hurdles in their law enforcement officer career quest.

July 2008
PoliceLink.com

10 Tips for Mastering the Police Oral Board

Oral boards are the key to getting hired. As a police academy manager and former police chief, I have seen countless applicants bomb their oral hiring board when they were otherwise good candidates. Like many other things in life, proper preparation can make the difference. This article will suggest ten tips to increase your chances for success.

1) Do your research. Study up on your target agency. In this age of the Internet, there is no excuse for walking into an agency without an intimate knowledge of its statistics and key personnel. Some items to glean off of the department and larger governmental entity (city, county, or state – not to mention airport, college, harbor, school district or other setting) websites are: population policed, agency chief executive (usually the elected sheriff or chief), divisions, number of law

enforcers, square miles of the jurisdiction, policing philosophy, and mission statement.

2) Be early. As the old saying goes: "early is on time and on time is late." I had the time that the person arrived for their oral board noted and relayed to me. My thought, along with many other chiefs, was that if the person can't make it on time (better yet early) for their interview when they should be on their best behavior, they certainly won't have good time management skills down the road when they are hired and off of their probationary status.

3) Check your appearance. Be sure that you are perceived as a professional. It should go without saying that all nose rings, tongue piercings, and earrings should be removed prior to coming into the area of the interview building. A dark suit with conservative tie and shirt is appropriate with men with similarly suitable business attire for women. Clothes should be cleaned and pressed. Oral board attendees should have their hygiene handled correctly. Special attention should be paid to nails and shoes.

4) Use proper titles. Make sure that you use the right titles when speaking at the oral board. Don't call a law enforcer an "officer" in a sheriff's office and vice versa (in that case, it should be "deputy sheriff"). Know the rank insignia for your target agency and the corresponding titles that go with them.

5) Know your elements. Some oral panels, particularly those that interview people who have already graduated

from a basic law enforcement academy, quiz the applicant on elements of common crimes. Know your state's criminal statutes and how they apply to situations. For example, you may be asked to define burglary or be presented with a situation, which comprise the legal components of burglary.

6) Make eye contact. Whether each member of the panel asks questions or only a facilitator speaks for the group, be sure to make eye contact with each person in the room. In the law enforcement world, the eye contact conveys confidence and respect.

7) Sound confident. Minimize the appearance of nervousness or a lack of confidence by practicing to avoid stuttering. Watch yourself in a mirror. Better yet, hold your own mock oral panel and videotape yourself. When you watch the tape later, you will catch both good and bad things that you did realize you were doing. Remember, we are our own harshest critics.

8) Avoid creating distractions. Distractions can come in the form of verbal cues (such as "um", "ok", and "see what I mean") or they can be physical (such as tapping a ring on the metal part of the chair). When distractions crop up, they make you appear nervous and detract from the message that you are trying to impart.

9) Plant your feet. Interview panel organizers frequently place the applicant in a swivel chair that also has the ability to recline. When you sit down, be sure to plant your feet and resist the inclination to swivel or

rock in the chair. Most panel members perceive movement in the chair as indicators of nervousness.

10) Shake hands. When an appropriate moment comes up, usually before exiting the interview room, stand up and walk over to each member of the panel. Address each by their rank or title and thank them individually for their time while shaking their hand.

These ten tips address some of the more blatant ones problems I have observed while running oral panels. As an applicant, you are granted around twenty minutes to give the panel members a glimpse of who you as a person and they type of law enforcer you would be if employed by the hiring agency.

Your first impression (commonly thought of as the first 15 seconds) as viewed by the panel members is crucial to the success of your oral board experience. Incorporate these ten tips as you thoroughly prepare for a pivotal, albeit brief, piece of the professional law enforcement officer application process.

August 2008
PoliceLink.com

Answering Common Oral Board Questions

My last Law Enforcement Career Expert column for PoliceLink.com covered ten tips for mastering the police oral board. This column covers how to answer the questions themselves. While I can't give you the exact wording that will work for you, understanding why certain questions are asked, and how to formulate the answer that fits you, is the key to getting hired in the competitive law enforcement hiring process. Of course that presumes that all political or favoritism issues are removed from the oral panel's judgment of the candidates.

As mentioned in the previous articles, as a police academy manager and former police chief, I have seen many people bomb that first impression formed at an oral board (usually within the first 15 seconds). Having been on both sides of the process as the interviewer and the interviewee (one large agency that I interviewed successfully with told me I scored the highest of any sworn applicant to that date – "Half a point away from a perfect score."), I have learned a few tricks that may help you. Some applicants may be well-dressed and appear sharp on oral board day, but when they open their mouth, it all goes out the window.

Here are some typical questions or concepts posed at oral panels and how to view them. Note that I could not possibly address all questions, but here are the more common ones that crop up. All of these broadly based answers will need to be refined by you to reflect the details that are unique to your life and circumstances.

The key here is to give an honest, heart-felt response that also falls within the acceptable broad parameters of oral interviews. Remember, oral board panels are made up of seasoned patrol officers and law enforcement executives. They are experienced, trained interviewers who are adept at ferreting out answers from people that are deceptive or not genuine.

1) Tell this panel about yourself. This is an open-ended statement, usually posed in the beginning, and it gives you a terrific opportunity to create that great first impression. It is also the point at which many people turn the panel members off. In the words of my good friend and recruiting guru Commander Mark Anderson, of the Altamonte Springs, FL, Police Department: "Tell me the time, don't build me a clock."

All too often the long-winded answer starts with: "Well, it all started 21 years ago when I was born in a small town..." The background sound everyone hears next is the snoring of the panel members. You should only hit the highlights that are relevant to their judging you as appropriate for the position. Relevant information includes education (college degree in criminal justice, etc.), work or volunteer experience (police explorer, sales or managerial experience, and military service), or family background and familiarization with the job (relatives or multiple generations that have served as police officers) that could be used to show your potential success as a law enforcement officer.

Practice your delivery of this brief, albeit important, synopsis of your life in front of a mirror or video camera. You may even want to hold a mock oral panel to hone your delivery and answers. Your answers, as with all of these panel responses, should be delivered with a confident tone that does not trail off at the end of each sentence. If they can't hear the end of your sentence, you convey the message that it's not worth hearing and consequently, they won't exert any effort to do so.

2) Why do you want to be a police officer/deputy sheriff/trooper? (Depending on the type of agency you are applying to) Try to avoid the cliché answers of "I want to serve and protect" or "I want to give back to the community." Cynical panel members are on the lookout for people who tell them what they think they want to hear.

I advise people, when you picture yourself as an officer, what is it that you are doing? If it is helping small children and being role model because the same thing occurred to you when you were a child interacting with a neighbor who was an officer, then say so. If it's because you've tried the indoor, office cubicle type of career path and you are looking for a more varied, outdoor type of excitement, then say so. If it's because you want to help bust drug dealers because your best friend from high school died after graduation from an overdose, then say so.

You have to help the panel understand that your desire stems from more than just the cars are pretty or you want to carry a gun and drive fast. Try not to focus solely on why the agency is good for you, but rather show the synergy between what you can bring to the agency and how that in turn will help you.

3) Why do you want to work for my agency? Here's where something more than the vague "it's the best department" is appropriate. You need to be more specific. First-hand knowledge of the agency that you have gained from doing ride-alongs or talking to the officers is crucial to helping you to come up with an answer that is truthful and works.

For example, maybe, after riding with a variety of agencies in your area, you were particularly impressed at how officers on a particular shift handled people at calls for police service with dignity and respect which reflects how you want to practice the art of policing. Or perhaps you found that the agency is heavy into DUI and traffic enforcement, which has meaning for you since a relative died from a drunk driver crash.

4) Tell me about a strength you have. This isn't something like I can "bench press 500 pounds." What about your character is illustrated in a trait? Are you a hard worker? Are you full of integrity and honor? Do you have a personal story that illustrates that trait in concrete terms?

5) Tell me about a weakness you have. What you need to do here is truthfully relate a weakness that in law enforcement circles is perceived actually as a virtue. For example, "I am a workaholic" or "I am sometimes too mission focused. I won't give up until the job is done." These might be problems if you were "interviewing" on a first date, but in the police world it is a nice fit.

We look for people whose weaknesses as perceived by the general population work in the challenging setting of policing in a democratic society. Someone that won't stop until the mission is accomplished is thought of as being obsessive in the general population, but is heralded as a survivor and winner in the police field.

6) Legal elements. If you have graduated already from a basic law enforcement academy, you may be hit with this item, as well as number seven below. You may be asked to list the elements of commonly encountered criminal law statutes. Be familiar with the elements or components that comprise burglary, robbery, and other crimes that officers contend with.

7) Legal concepts. Be able to explain legal concepts. Be sure that you understand them and are not just regurgitating a definition from a textbook or statute book. For example, can you define the difference between reasonable suspicion and probable cause, as well as misdemeanor and felony?

8) Policing concepts. Be familiar with the policing concepts that drive your target agency. A read of their website (which hopefully is up to date) and materials in the lobby should clue you as to their approach. Are they community policing oriented? If so, they may ask you what community policing means to you. Understand their website's interpretation, but personalize it in terms of what it means to you. Figure out if the agency is proactive or reactive in their approach to calls for police service.

An area that comes up in some oral boards concerns the use of deadly force. Be familiar with not only your area's statutory requirements for the use of deadly force, but also think through the ethical and moral implications for yourself. By reflecting on this tragic but oftentimes present aspect of your chosen profession, you'll be a more mature candidate for the post.

There are many more questions or statements that oral panels put out for applicants to respond to, including ethical situations. This column addressed some of the more common ones that you might encounter.

I have seen firsthand how practicing your responses to these oral panel situations have led to dramatic improvement. While I don't advocate a memorized approach, being familiar in general with how to respond will free you to have a compelling delivery that will captivate the panel members. It is at that point, that they will have a feel for your character and the sort of law enforcer that you can be for their agency. A good oral panel interview will help you to get that opportunity.

Dr. Richard Weinblatt

September 2008
PoliceLink.com

Getting hired: It's all about the patterns

With all of the articles, emails, discussions that I participate in on getting hired by law enforcement agencies, it becomes clear that a person's hirability is not in the stars. Rather, it comes down to patterns. Police chiefs, sheriffs, and their designees in the forms of recruiters and background investigators, are looking for patterns. As a police chief, I did likewise and I still see this in my current role helping Seminole Community College police academy graduates to land their coveted badge. This article for PoliceLink.com covers what those often highlighted patterns are to help you to ascertain and manage your own patterns in your bid to get hired.

While law enforcement contacts and networking help in many places - the old "who you know..." theory - (that's a topic for another, upcoming article), this article deals with those patterns of behavior that agency executives use to predict future performance. Simply put: agencies are looking for patterns of responsibility and patterns of irresponsibility. It is important to bear in mind that some agencies are stricter in their scrutiny of patterns than others. Generally, I have found the larger agencies to be tougher in excusing patterns of irresponsibility than those who are smaller and tend to be located in more rural areas where the applicant pool may not be as plentiful or draw from a nationwide base.

A pattern of responsibility is what background investigators like to see. More specifically, they want all of the end documentation in the file to reflect a pattern of responsibility. That pattern can emerge in one area, though it is preferred to see it cross over multiple facets of an applicant's life.

One area they examine is the academic patterns. A red flag that I've seen many times is an academic transcript riddled with "F"s. Even worse may be an academic record that has many "W"s indicating a pattern of withdrawing or completing a task anytime it becomes difficult. LE executives see this as behavior that will continue when their uniform is put on. On the flipside, "A"s are not necessary (although it is nice), but a pattern of "A"s and "B"s shows someone who is consistent in their effort to do their best and not give up on a task prior to its completion.

Another area they examine is job stability. Whether the applicant has had one job or several jobs, they want stability to be reflected in the person's employment history. A recent applicant to area law enforcement agencies had some 23 jobs in 26 years. This young man has had a hard time getting hired. Some of those slots were held for barely a month. Given the quest for applicants with long-term job stability, it is also understood by most investigators that certain industries (such as construction and restaurant workers) experience a higher turnover than other fields and allowances are often made accordingly.

The quality of military service and the type of discharge given to a military veteran applicant is also examined. A copy of the DD-214 is standard supporting documentation mandated with applications. Most police chiefs and sheriffs are military veterans who come from an era of military service. They understandably take such service to the nation seriously, as well as the applicant's personal characteristics represented by the applicant's military evaluations, commendations, and discharge paperwork. A little digging here by the background investigator may reveal a pattern of dishonesty, psychological instability, or just plain laziness.

Patterns of financial responsibility also come into the picture. It is important to have pattern of being fiscally responsible with your personal finances. Contrary to what many have asked me, debt is not the issue. The problem comes in when that debt is not being regularly paid to the lender according to an agreed upon payback schedule. Doing so shows a pattern of living up to one's word and legal obligations.

Driving has gained a news level of importance as governmental entities face pressure from their insurance carriers. Officers, deputy sheriffs, and state troopers spend more time behind the wheel of potentially lethal vehicles than in any other high liability area. An applicant's driving record has been sued in many cases as the deal breaker that cost them the conditional job offer. A pattern of irresponsible driving as evidenced by multiple citations will not sit nicely under the chief's scrutiny.

Like-wise a criminal record, even a minor one that shows evidence of being a repeated occurrence will bode poorly for the aspiring badge bearer. Some states, such as Florida, stop the process if even one felony pops up. Some agencies may be open to minor transgressions, especially if they are honestly disclosed during the applicant process and happened some time ago, but all of that goes out of the window if the type of incident is repeated several times.

Minor drug usage follows the same line of thinking. Again, agencies are looking for a pattern. However, serious drug use, even one time, may disqualify the applicant in some jurisdictions (depending on local policies).

All of these patterns of behavior are examined (as well as a few others not mentioned here,). To the law enforcement hiring executive who is cognizant of his or her role in avoiding negligent hiring liability and picking the applicant most likely to serve well, an examination of the patterns serve as indicators of future performance as a sworn law enforcer.

An honest, self-appraisal of patterns you may have, along with a behavior adjustment to halt the bad ones and highlight the good ones, will enhance your chances of being hired by the agency of your choice. The answer, oh job applicant, is not in the stars; it is in the patterns.

January 2009
PoliceLink.com

Bad Credit, Bad Applicant

Many folks applying for law enforcement jobs fret about such possible background issues as criminal history or driving record, but few consider the impact their credit report can have on them. Given the current national focus on economic and credit issues, the topic is particularly timely.

To start to understand how police background investigators, recruiters, police chiefs and sheriffs view an applicant's credit, it is important to understand what it is and how a person's action, or inaction, can affect the credit score. The three main credit-reporting bureaus (Equifax, Experian, and TransUnion) use a number to help banks and other lenders to assess a borrower's risk and, if a loan is approved, what interest rate to charge.

The number they used, called a FICO score (from the Fair Isaac Company) is derived from five categories – owed amounts, payment history, length of credit history, age of credit, and type of credit utilized (credit cards are looked at more than mortgages, for instance). Credit scores range from a low of 300 up the high 800s.

Police academy students have asked me if the ads for companies offering to clean up bad credit are above board. The true medicine for an ill credit report is time and consistency in paying owed amounts on time.

So why should an applicant worry about their credit history and FICO score? Because the administrators reviewing the application are concerned with that aspect of your life. As I mentioned in my previous PoliceLink.com article "Getting Hired: It's About the Patterns, they look for patterns; patterns of responsibility and patterns of irresponsibility. That sounds a lot like the way your FICO scored is figured.

Background investigators generally are not concerned if there is some reasonable debt in your life. They just want to be sure that you are consistently honoring your obligation towards that debt. The approach demonstrates the trait of responsibility that they believe will also become evident when you get hired as a law enforcer. The concept is along the lines of the old background investigator adage that goes something like this: "past behavior is a reliable indicator of future performance."

While law enforcement agencies have long looked to credit as a part of the background packet, other employers are using the same tactic and even insurance companies have jumped on the bandwagon. All see it as an indicator of how someone has lived their life thus far and will continue to do so.

Law enforcement agencies also reason that someone with pressing financial issues may be tempted to solicit a bribe or swipe some cash during an open door residential alarm house search. The opportunities for ill-gotten gain are ever present in law enforcement. LE executives see someone with large financial pressures as not being able to resist the temptations as much as someone who has minimal economic concerns.

So, you ask, how can a bad credit score be fixed? Much like the drunk driver that thinks coffee will help them sober up, only time and good behavior can clean up the financial house. Consistently paying on time and eliminating particularly credit card debt is the path to take. Early steps such as using a secured, pre-paid credit card will help in the recovery from a bad credit score or worse, a bankruptcy.

On the other hand, not having credit cards or any loans outstanding can also give you a low credit score due to a lack of a pattern or credit history. Many young applicants to police agencies run into this issue as they still live with their parents and drive a car that is in their parents' name. These youthful applicants need to get some form of easily obtained credit (such as a department store credit card) and demonstrate responsibility by dutifully paying the credit card company on time. That will help them build up their FICO credit score.

As the economy continues to squeeze local governmental revenue sources, law enforcement executives have gotten pickier with the applicants they choose to hire. What used to be a seller's market is now a buyer's market that favors the agencies. More segments of our society are viewing law enforcement as a steady employer in uncertain times. Credit scores are another indicator that police departments and sheriff's offices use to ensure that only the most qualified of applicants are culled from the pack.

August 2009
PoliceLink.com

Behind the Scenes at Police Oral Boards

In previous PoliceLink.com career expert columns, I have delved into how to answer oral board questions and position your honest answers in the best light possible. This column will take you behind the scenes and explore how interview panels are constructed and what hiring administrators are really trying to find out in oral boards. By understanding how they are designed and what they are looking for, you will be better prepared to present a positive image and thus be more appealing for hire.

In order to understand what they are trying to do, you have to comprehend the basic types of panels that are utilized. As we have vastly different police departments and sheriff's offices around the nation, so too does that divergence reflect in the way oral interview panels are constructed, convened, and executed. There are many variations, so we will cover the main ones and the corresponding concerns of executives.

Old School, Adversarial Oral Panel

Adversarial oral boards are the older version of today's more prevalent and more civil panel. In an adversarial oral panel interview, the applicant is subjected to various techniques designed to make him or her nervous. The aim is to see how they operate under pressure and try to predict if they would do so if hired as a law enforcement officer.

A major problem came in years ago in that, due to the subjective nature of the unplanned questioning, unsuccessful applicants could allege unfair or disparate treatment. This was a particularly powerful argument when it came to females and minorities.

The applicant under this model is made to wait past their scheduled interview time. This is done on purpose to create anxiety. When the interviewee is finally brought in the room, he or she is seated in a swivel chair placed far away from the interview panel in a lonely area of the floor. Panel members are uniformed and remain stone faced even in when humor is introduced into the answers.

This version not used by many agencies anymore, calls for an unscripted or loosely scripted series of questions. Whatever the answer provided, the panel members are free to follow up with questions that are often challenging in nature. Again, the goal is to see if the applicant changes his or her answers or cracks under the pressure. They watch to see if the applicant nervously swivels the chair and otherwise display physical mannerisms that telegraph a lack of confidence.

For a variety of reasons, including the lack of legal defensibility, I do not encourage agencies to use this model of oral panels anymore. Thankfully, most have jettisoned it for a more polite, standardized version. Human resources folks correctly shudder at this incarnation of an oral panel.

Standardized Oral Panel

The standardized oral panel is the more widely used interview vehicle in law enforcement today. Under this model, each and every applicant is asked the same series of standardized questions. Human resources professionals have vetted these questions to exclude any that are discriminatory, arbitrary, subjective, or would otherwise expose the agency or the governmental entity to liability.

Each panel member may ask questions in a set sequence. Alternately, one facilitator (usually someone who is the ranking officer) will ask the questions on behalf of the panel. In both cases, the members will have the questions on a photocopied sheet in front of them with room to write notes and place a score.

It is not unusual for the panelists to appear to be stone faced. That is part of the plan. They do this to 1) not betray any bias for one candidate over another one, and

2) to take you out of your comfort zone. They want to see if you'll stick with your answer and display confidence in the face of a possible challenge. This is much like an officer has to.

Informal Chat Interview

Some agencies have gone an even newer route of interviews in a more informal setting. In this scenario, the candidate is seated at the table with the panel members who are still armed with pre-determined, standardized questions

The emphasis here is not so much to see how the applicant reacts under stress, but to disarm him or her so they give more honest answers. The feeling is that an uncomfortable atmosphere breeds on guard answers. Those who advocate this informal approach see it as a way to lull the person into a sense of security so that ostensibly the answers become more genuine.

This type of interview is also engineered to be able to get a sense of your personality. They want to see you in a more relaxed atmosphere to see if you have a sense of humor and can get along with their people and their corporate culture.

Placement

For some agencies, this is the first step in the process. For others, it may be placed later in the process when certain background material is available for the panel to incorporate within their prepared questions. In either situation, the questions are designed to elicit responses that would give the panel a view as to whether the person would be a good fit for their agency.

And this is an important point. Oral panels often reflect the corporate culture of the agency. Both their construction and their interpretation of the applicant's answers depend greatly on the values and approach of the agency leadership. As I have told many graduates of the police academies I run, just because they did make it through the oral panel selection to go on to the next phase in the hiring process, does not mean they would make a bad law officer; rather it may just mean that they were not the right fit for that particular agency.

August 2009
PoliceLink.com

Ten Tips to Get Kicked out of the Police Academy

Alright, so now that you've attained your hard fought for goal of getting into the police academy, you want to continue to be goal oriented and get kicked out. If that's your new goal, here are ten sure fire ways to get the boot. These career-killing moves could also apply to your future position as a law enforcement officer after the academy.

1) Lie. It's a simple, one word activity. You could lie on your entrance application. You could lie in a conversation with the academy director or commander. You could omit information when asked about a fellow cadets alleged exam cheating. No matter how you slice it, it speaks to your lack of integrity and it is a sure fire way to get the axe.

I get asked all the time why honesty and integrity are such big issues for law enforcement. Why? Because people went to prison for years based sometimes solely on my word. A law enforcer's honor can't be negotiable because the stakes are so high for people in our society. A professional law enforcement officer's credibility is key to their solid relationship with the courts, fellow officers, and the public.

2) Go naked. Or otherwise don't conform to the published policies governing hygiene and uniform standards. You could not shave. That gets you sent home for sure. You also could "forget" to clean and press your academy uniform. You could wear white socks when you're not supposed to. Hey, then you'll like an old episode of COPS. Keep that up, and you'll be watching the show instead of living it.

3) Be drunk and use drugs. Since you're in the academy, you could feel that you don't have to live that clean lifestyle anymore. You could go out boozin' and druggin' at late night parties. After all, it's outside of academy hours.

4) Sexually harass. Most academies have strict policies covering sexual harassment. And invariably I have, as well as commanders working for me, had to address the topic on an individual basis. The courts have held supervisory staff responsible for curtailing such activities, so they are unlikely to look the other way or protect you from getting the heave ho.

So if you're an academy squad leader, make sure to get that quid pro quo (something for something in return) from one of your squad members. Or you could bring in that centerfold nude picture and put it on the podium. Or you could trick a new instructor into playing a sexually provocative video in front of the class. Those will get ya out the door for sure.

5) Don't study. Academies tend to be made up of block exams. In some you have to fail three and you're gone. In others, it's less. If you want to be bye bye real quick, ignore the academy staff's admonitions to study for the exams. Besides knowing all those laws and policing concepts aren't helpful to be a cop anyway.

6) Refuse PT. In some states, exit physical fitness standards are set in concrete by the state. For example, in Ohio some 40% of cadets statewide fail the exit physical fitness standards and are therefore not able to sit for the state exam. They are done at that point. There is no debate and they are sent packin'.

Physical fitness in policing is not just important because of state certification standards; the small issue like your life may depend on it enters into the picture. But go ahead and ignore all that. Be lazy. Refuse to do PT. I'm sure that they'll give you a ride to your car.

7) Talk back. Given that former police chiefs with military backgrounds run most academies, insubordination is a great way to get in hot water. And be sure that the command that you refuse to follow is both lawful and ethical so you have no grounds upon which to object later when you are in the director's office.

8) Be late or absent. Much like the lottery where you have to be in it to win it, you'll need to be in the chair to get through the academy. In your bid to get tossed out, you could come late repeatedly and hey, why not just go fishing.

Academies have attendance requirement mandates placed on them by the state certification entities. Beyond their own organizational attendance mandates, academy honchos have to answer to higher authorities regarding the cadets' seat time. Being AWOL and skipping class is sure to get their attention.

9) Bring guns. Especially for academies that are housed within college institutions, bringing your favorite canon to show your fellow academy students gives you a great shot at being ejected. And it's against the law too. Which brings us to the big one…

10) Break the law. Taking the criminal law block gives you all sorts of neat ways to break the law. You could test your theory as to whether those in (or entering) the police profession are above the law.

All of the above, especially the last one, are not recommended paths for academy success. On the contrary, they are the antithesis of what good professional law enforcement should be about. The academy portion of your development as a professional is geared to be a microcosm of your life in an employing agency.

The academy is the time to perfect skills and display a positive, excited attitude. The future is yours to have- unless you're looking to get the boot.

August 25, 2009
PoliceOne.com

Top 10 social networking tips for cops

In the wake of the widely known Texas waitress photos which led to the firing of one Midland County deputy sheriff and the suspension of three others, a look at how online technology has impacted the world of the law enforcement officer seemed to be warranted. This is not a new occurrence. Recall if you will the Hoboken, NJ, SWAT team disbanded following "racy" Hooters girl pictures bearing weaponry on police vehicles. The self-replicating Internet made sure that everyone eventually saw the pictures in question.

As someone who oversees Basic Police Academies, currently in Ohio and previously in Florida, I have long advised students on the benefits of the wise use of an online persona. While some officers totally bypass any use of online sites in a bid to protect themselves in the future, I view that as throwing the baby out with the bath water. I advocate a more controlled use of those outlets.

I personally make much use of technology having accounts on a variety of websites including Facebook, Twitter, MySpace, youtube, Blogger, and Linkedin among others. I have for many years, including when I served as a police chief, with no negative consequences.

These are useful tools for personal and professional networking and communication. I use the analogy that any tool, including firearm and Taser, can be abused. It is the professional officer that knows how to use these technology tools responsibly and in accordance with departmental policies and community morals.

Many officers have forfeited an otherwise promising career for a few moments of posting euphoria. While other folks may garner only a chuckle in response to their online adventures, a professional law enforcer is held to a higher standard by most employing agencies.

The phenomenal growth of technological innovation has impacted law enforcement from the advent of digital photography to the omnipresent social network Facebook. This article offers tips for using the new online technologies while not sacrificing your career.

1) No gun glorification. While this may upset the Second Amendment supporters out there, the reality is that many of the public does not like to see a glorification of firearms in pictures of law enforcers. Quite a few officers have lost their jobs after posing

with weaponry in a way perceived as offensive or too warrior oriented.

While the depiction of guns in the course of their normal scope and use is not problematic, aiming the gun at the camera seems to be the trigger for the pink slip. Shots of officers engaged in their normal course of fire at the gun range have not appeared to bring about a backlash. Posing with weaponry, involving either the officer or (worse yet) a civilian, has historically been problematic for the employee.

2) No alcohol. Officers have also found themselves in the hot seat after posting pictures of them partying and drinking alcohol. Many agencies view this to be contrary to a professional image. Of even more concern is that sometimes others identified in the pictures turn out to be minors in possession of alcohol which itself opens up another can of issues.

3) Watch your comments. This is an important one. Posted comments on social networking sites are being dragged into legal proceedings especially when use of force is involved. Comments that imply the officer enjoys using force on people, especially certain groups of people, are being seized on by criminal defense and civil plaintiffs' attorney to show the officer had a pre disposition to be physical or has a documented bias against their client.

Be mindful that discussion boards and the like are a public written record of your communication. Like reports and radio dispatch conversations, they can be discovered and frame your actions in a context that you may not like. Much like reports, if you don't want it dragged into the legal arena, don't type it online.

4) Avoid department bashing. Another area that has gotten some officers into hot water, the First Amendment freedom of speech notwithstanding, are comments that bash the agency. Depending on how it is framed, it could open you up to administrative charges and possibly civil liability. More and more bloggers and online posters are being held responsible for their critical speech online. Especially if it is later proved that the postings lack a factual basis and are intended to damage the target of the criticism.

At the very least, launching such a site or contributing to an existing website that bashes the agency does not endear you to the powers that be or position you as a team player ripe for promotion.

5) Restrict personal information. Much like we can use Facebook and the like as a tool to find people and research information, so too can the bad guys. Be judicious in the posting of information and pictures. For example, some officers will not use pictures of their family members or going even further, of themselves. Others, like me, withhold their cell phone number.

6) Picture Choice. Make sure that the pictures that you do choose to post don't have any of the aforementioned problem areas or have nudity. Many officers, including myself, have shirtless bodybuilding or fitness oriented photos online. That is not a problem. The topless

woman drinking at the party with you exemplifies what is a problem.

7) Minimize status update complaints. In this ear of economic contraction, there are many people waiting in line for your spot in the agency. Administrators know this. We've all seen the officers that post their status with complaints about the shift, their sergeant, or the job. I've heard some supervisors who state, after reading such negatively tinged status updates, let so and so "find another job if they are so unhappy here."

While not every job is going to be great each and every day, gripes should not be aired via status updates. The agency may only be too happy to find someone else that would appreciate them.

8) Highlight accomplishments. Many look to Facebook, Linkedin, and the like as electronic resumes. Take advantage of that and use it to highlight your professional accomplishments. Post pictures of you learning some new technique (being careful not to show scores or other information). Post status updates of that advanced training course you take.

9) Set privacy settings. While I have my online presence open to the public, many have privacy settings that restrict access to family and friends that you have predetermined. While not foolproof, the settings should keep most interlopers locked out of your pages.

10) When in doubt, leave it out. I have long coached academy students and officers to pretend that I am

perched on their shoulder and watching what they are doing. In the same vein, they could have their mother hovering overhead. If you wouldn't want us to see it or if either of us would be displeased with what is being contemplated to go online, it probably is not a good idea to upload it.

September 2009
PoliceLink.com

Ten Tips for On Target Academy Firearms Training

The prospect of firearms training in the pressure filled basic law enforcement academy setting is either loved or hated by cadets. Few blocks of instruction, save for physical training and defensive tactics, conjures up such extremes in emotion. As a certified firearms instructor and an executive over basic police academies, I have seen first-hand the issues that trip up aspiring gun-toting law enforcers. This "Law Enforcement Career Expert" column on PoliceLink.com has been crafted to offer firearms training bound recruits tips for success using a vital tool of the professional law enforcer.

1) Automatic Safety. The cardinal concept of firearms training is that of safety. Academies routinely distribute a document containing rules of safety on the police

firing range. Most have the students read, sign, and return the document. Find out what those rules are in advance and be sure to be familiar which each important mandate. Make compliance with such standard rules as "assume every firearm is loaded," "Never point the firearm at something that you don't want to shoot," and "be aware of what your target is and beyond" automatic. Not having to apply thought to those mandates are frees you to concentrate on the psycho motor skills needed for excellent marksmanship.

2) Strength Training. A major problem that detracts from working on shooting skills is a lack of upper body strength. Effecting particularly small-framed men and women, handguns made heavier with ammunition and long guns such as shotguns strain and distracts struggling shooters from refining their skills.

3) No "Windage." Often when firearms instructors do some target analysis and point out where the grouping of rounds are hitting the paper troubled shooters decide that simply moving the grouping by compensating with the front site is the solution. Referred to as the "windage" method by seasoned firearms instructors, this is not a true solution and really cheats the student shooter of developing good trigger control skills. For example, if the right-handed shooter is mashing the trigger and target analysis sees this manifested as the grouping falling low and to the left. The "windage" shooter places the front sight high and to the right of the target area to improperly compensate.

4) Don't have mind of your own. Many instructors get frustrated by recruits that ask for help on the line, get it, and then go back to what they were doing wrong. Different firearms instructors will make divergent suggestions. Try them out and see what works best for you. Problems come in when students go back to their own flawed ways once the instructor shifts the focus from them to another student. Listen to the firearms instructors and try it their way.

5) Don't rely on gadgets. Many struggling shooters feel that they would do better if only they had a particular flashlight, laser, grip or other firearm accoutrement. The fact is, while the gadgetry is nice, it's the shooter behind the gun, not the gun, that truly makes the difference.

6) Mixed Dummy Rounds and dry fire. Students often anticipate the gun firing and firearms instructors working the firing line can clearly peg the students who are scared of that round going off. There are several old tricks that I and other instructors use to solve the issue. One is to mix dummy rounds in with the live ball ammo in the magazine. This is done out of sight of the cadet so that he or she will not know which rounds are live and which are not. When the student gets up to one of the dummy rounds in the magazine, they see for themselves the front of the muzzle going down. Often seeing for themselves is more powerful and effective than us verbally explaining it.

7) Dry Fire. Along the same vein as number six, dry firing the weapon is actually more helpful and can be

done by most recruits at home. Assuming that the cadet has their firearm available at home and that they have visually and physically checked and determined that the firearm is unloaded, they can place a penny just behind the front sight. Some weapons, such as Glocks, will necessitate a slight slide movement to re-engage the trigger. The recruit picks a spot on the wall or the TV and carefully squeezes the trigger with the aim being not to move or drop the penny off the top of the slide. Repeating this step numerous times goes a long way towards establishing muscle memory and minimizing weapon movement while maximizing trigger and breath control, as well as sight alignment.

8) Control fear. Whether it is the noise, the recoil, the orange muzzle flash, or some people's discomfort with weaponry, many people are afraid of the firearm that they need to master. Contrary to what we all see in the movies or on TV, folks don't fly ten feet back when shot. By the same token, shooters do not fly back either. Many shooters lean forward dramatically anticipating a large amount of kick from the weapon when it is discharged. The laws of physics make sure that the kick is not huge.

9) Eat, drink, and dress appropriately. Ranges, particularly outdoor ranges can be environmentally tough locations. Many firearms instructors feel that police officers and deputy sheriffs are required to police in all weather conditions and thus so too should police academy students. Short of lightning, most academies shoot in rain, snow, sand storms, and other weather related hardships. Be sure to check the weather report

and dress appropriately within the academy uniform standards. For example, if it is cold, you may want to have long johns under your academy uniform.

By the same token, low blood sugar from a lack of proper nutrition will not improve your shootings scores. Be sure to eat and drink properly over the long term.

10) Front sight focus. One of things that I did myself during qualifications is to say out loud (but softly) "front sight, front sight. Front sight, squeeze." This forces me to concentrate on the front sight and squeeze until the round goes down range. That same method has given students of mine a good start in their firearms oriented career.

Whether you are a die-hard second amendment supporter or a reluctant gun toter, firearms are part of the tools available to officers. Following these ten tips should help you to alleviate any stress-related firearms training and become more proficient with firearms.

March 11, 2010
PoliceLink.com

10 Tricks for Picking the Right Department

One of the most common questions I get overseeing criminal justice and police academies is from students who want to know what law enforcement agency they should apply to. The answer is not so simple. There have long been a variety of factors to consider when deciding where to apply. That has only been more complicated by the downturn in the economy that has turned the justice job arena from a seller's market to a buyer's market.

The job market has only become tougher as the law of supply and demand has reversed from a few years when there were more slots than applicants. Now, there are more applicants than slots. While finding the best-qualified folks is still a challenge for police chiefs and sheriffs, it certainly is easier than it has been before.

Police work is now looked upon as a steady occupation with good benefits. That is something that has become scarce for many people in this challenging economy. The numbers of those applying for police posts has skyrocketed, particularly for destination agencies that are desirable due to their reputation or location (such as Florida).

Much like the private sector, governmental entities have been impacted with shrinking revenue bases upon which to build their police personnel pools. Worse yet for those contemplating a career move into the five-0 biz is the way governmental funding cycles work. Despite what may seem to a gradual improvement in the economy, many see the next few years as being even rougher than 2010 as onetime federal stimulus funds from the Obama administration will dry up. Tax and other governmental revenue cycles for state and local public agencies also almost always trail that of the private sector.

There are some folks I have spoken with that advocate what I'll call the shotgun approach to law enforcement applications. This has been especially true due to the desperation caused by the above factors. I do not advocate that approach. I liken that approach to applying for credit. If you get turned down a bunch of times, any prospective creditors see those many declinations and wonder why and if they should dig further.

It the same principle behind gas station clerks parking their own car at a gas pump later at night to simulate other folks being comfortable being a customer of that establishment. If too many folks bypass the gas station (and no one is there) or you are turned down by many agencies, any prospective target is going to want to go where others would want to go.

So, the idea is to pick wisely. Here are five tips to help you do so.

1) Figure out who is hiring. No amount of your personal desire will get you a coveted position if that agency isn't hiring. Worse yet, is the situation where hiring happens followed shortly thereafter by the layoff of the lowest seniority probationary employees due to budget cuts.
The idea is to take a proactive research approach to get a handle on both scenarios. Find out from instructors and other law enforcers in your social and professional network who is looking to take on new officers. Scour the classified ads, sites like PoliceLink.com, and jib search boards like Monster.com.

In order to make sure you landing in an economically viable agency that won't likely turn around and lay you off quickly, I suggest that you research the city or county finances. Check council minutes, scrutinize public financial records, and read relevant newspaper articles online.

2) Figure out the type of policing you want to do. Different types of law enforcement agencies represent divergent categories of police work. If your bag is traffic enforcement and crash investigation, than a state

police/highway patrol/state patrol type of agency may be the ticket for you. If you like to have a little more independence and little backup, than a county sheriff in a geographically far flung county may be good for you. If you want a slower pace with a community feel, then a small town with low call volume may be right.

But don't forget the many other types of law enforcement out there. Community policing has long traditionally had a strong presence in campus law enforcement. Railroad aficionados may think that railroad police is the track for them. And outdoor buffs may find being a wildlife enforcement officer is the branch for them.

3) Check the website. It sounds obvious, but many people I speak with have yet to even check the agency's website. A lot of information can be gleaned from the department's Internet presence. Many agencies have terrific websites with all sorts of information and even recruitment videos.

4) Google and youtube. Yet another one that I think is obvious that few do. Google the department to find out what information is out there. Go a step further and Google them again under the "news" tab to see what news articles have popped up recently.

Another great Internet resource is youtube.com. Pull up youtube and do a search with the agency name. You may find official recruitment videos, as well as grainy cell phone camera footage of their officers in action. Bearing in mind that footage can be misleading depending what the poster wants viewers to see, it can give you further insight on the agency.

5) Do ride-alongs. Nothing gets you a feel for any agency as much as actually sitting in the car and watching the types and volume of calls for service, attitude of the sworn personnel, and support given to the street officers (someone you are hoping to be) by the administration. The world is different on the other side of the windshield. Just remember, while you are checking out the agency, they are scrutinizing you. This is especially true if they know you have already applied to them. It is a chance for you to get information and to impress, but it can also be a chance to ruin your reputation if you say or do inappropriate things during the ride-along.

6) Check out your instructors. Many of your adjunct criminal justice degree and basic police academy instructors are full-time or retired members of local law enforcement agencies. Figure out if you like their approach to policing and if their level of professionalism matches that of which you'd like to see in your future hiring agency. However, much like the ride-alongs above, they are checking you out as much as you are they.

7) Turn-over. Ask or research what's happening with the personnel in the agency. The sick leave rate and turnover of personnel will give you a major clue as to the level of employee satisfaction. If many folks leave the agency, the next question revolves around the why. Is it due to low pay? Is it due to an oppressive

management culture? Is it due to inordinately high call volume? Or is it because of a cultural aversion to training or continuing education?

8) Equipment. What is an attraction to many, particularly as they start out in law enforcement, (not to seem flippant) are the toys of the profession. However, there is another reason to pay attention to the "toys."

The amount and quality of the cars, firearms, uniforms, and other accoutrements are great indicators of the financial, tactical, and moral commitment that the employing agency makes to their officers. Departments that issue a full complement of top shelf equipment to new officers underscore their financial stability and moral agreement that they have a vested interest in the tactical physical and emotional well-being of their community guardians.

9) If after all of the above, you are still not sure, you can explore becoming a reserve or volunteer sworn and certified police officer or deputy sheriff. Depending on your state and local jurisdiction laws and policies, you may be fully sworn and fully deployed, or you may have more a support role.

In either scenario, many agencies hire their full-time officers from the pool of reserve officers. The reason is simple. While you are getting a closer look at the agency, they get an opportunity to see you in action over time and don't have to pay you for the FTO ride time and related expenses such as benefits usually incurred with full-time employees.

10) Philosophy. This is harder to nail down, but is ultimately more important than all of the above. While mission statements and organizational values are posted on their website, they don't always reflect the reality that rolls out on the streets. A combination of the above should give you a good indicator.

The reason this is important is because your budding philosophy of how the art of policing should be practiced may be at odds with an agency that employs you. It is not a situation that lends itself to your success in the field training officer (FTO) program, nor will it be fulfilling.

For example, if you are a community minded prospective public servant, working for an agency that in reality sees the public as the enemy and practices an "us vs. them" mentality will result in a the philosophical clash that will undermine your view of the profession and career success.

I caution new entrants in the field from bypassing one agency for another for a two thousand dollar salary differential. That is not such an important deciding factor. The difference between agencies spread out over a year and after taxes is minimal. What will make more of a difference in your daily life is your happiness and philosophical compatibility with the employing law enforcement agency.

It is important for you, within the acknowledged context of a tighter job market, to pick your employing law enforcement agency as carefully as they pick you. Much like a marriage, it is a big step reflecting a commitment of a lifetime and a shared value and philosophical system. Take the time reflective of such a serious responsibility so you can best serve yourself, your family, and your community.

Dr. Richard Weinblatt

April 6, 2010
PoliceLink.com

10 Tips for Ride-Alongs

Popular among law enforcers, aspiring officers, spouses of officers, dispatchers, community activists, journalists, and scholars, ride-alongs with on-duty police officers and deputy sheriffs have long been a fun-filled way to get a view from the other side of a particular department's windshield. Whether you are exploring the idea of a career in law enforcement, wanting a closer look at your local constabulary, or seeking that quality time with your fellow law enforcer or significant other, ride-alongs can be a positive learning experience that strengthens bonds, but can also be fraught with pitfalls.

Not all law enforcement agencies have ride-along programs. Those that do, view it as a powerful bridge to the community. Those that don't usually believe the liability issues in having civilians present in dangerous situations are too high. Some agencies do permit the practice, but may restrict it to certain types of folks. Examples of the people that may be allowed to participate include dispatchers, police officer job applicants, enrolled police academy cadets, criminal justice college students, college interns, or spouses of officers.

While riding along with a law enforcement agency can be fun, make no mistake about it. Ride-alongs are a dangerous activity. There have been instances of ride-alongs being present when officers are attacked and they witness other harsh realities of policing in America. This is not the sanitized TV version of COPS.

By the way, sworn officers sometimes participate in ride-along programs. They may want to ride with a friend in another agency in order to bond further or they may be interested in learning different police practices and operations. It is important that officers follow their department's and the host agency's policies as far as carrying weaponry and taking action to assist the on-duty officer. There are jurisdictional differences in laws and protocols that greatly affect how the guest officer conducts him or herself on the ride-along.

Suggestions geared to civilian ride-alongs obviously don't apply to sworn law enforcement personnel riding off-duty with other agencies or divisions within their department. Whatever the case, make sure you know your boundaries from the agency and the individual officer before you step into the car.

Having managed ride-along programs, had ride-alongs with me as a full-timer, and ridden along with officers in other agencies in the United States and overseas, I have picked up a few tips to help make your ride-along a more productive and enjoyable experience.

1) Do Paperwork. Ride-alongs in almost every agency I have ever seen involve the filling out of at least some paperwork. That paperwork usually encompasses a liability waiver that needs to be signed. Some agencies do allow minors to ride-along and those add a signature line for a parent or guardian. You may also have to read, agree to, and sign a departmental policy or booklet on ride-along rules. Other paperwork includes information and permission to run name, driver's license operator number, social security number, and date of birth information through law enforcement databases. Make sure that all of the information provided is true and correct. This paperwork facilitates conducting of an at least cursory background check. Law enforcement folks certainly don't want convicted or wanted criminals riding next to their officers.

2) Clear Up Warrants. And speaking of background checks, make sure that any warrants you may have are cleared up prior to applying for a ride-along. The police are not fond of wanted criminals riding with them, so they do check.

You laugh at the thought that someone would do this with an active warrant in the system, but I recall one young man that had requested permission to do a ride-along. Well, you can guess that his background check

---

came up with a warrant for failure to appear (for court). I called him up and told him to come to the building, as his ride-along was ready. So, being a service-minded public servant, he got his ride-along as he wished-except it was in the back seat, not in the front seat. And it was only to the county jail. He even got a close up feel for handcuffs.

3) Wear Appropriate Clothing in Layers. As a ride-along in a marked police car, many folks will assume that you are some kind of detective or otherwise affiliated with the agency. You want to dress professionally, but still geared for a dynamic environment. I suggest business casual with comfortable shoes in the off chance you need to run out of the area. No shorts or jeans with holes or T-shirts (especially with questionable graphics or wording on it). Do not wear clothing articles with law enforcement logos or graphics. A collared polo shirt or button down shirt with khaki pants is appropriate.

Because officers wear bullet resistant vests, they tend to run hot, so they crank up the air-conditioning. As a result the front of the car can get quite cold. The use of layered clothing allows you to regulate your comfort without infringing on the officer. There can also be quite a temperature difference from being inside the car to being outside the vehicle. The use of layered clothing enables you to manage that issue as well.

4) Don't Touch Radios, Computer, etc. Most officers will give you a tour of the car when you start the shift. Very importantly, they'll show you the radio that is

their lifeline to communications. As the officers and telecommunicators in PoliceLink-land know, the dispatcher is an important person to the responding law enforcer. If they are in trouble, the radio is the conduit for getting help.

Don't play with the radio or change the frequency channel. Officers are very protective of the controls in their "cockpit." If they do instruct you to call for help, or you have to do so when they can't, press the button on the side of the microphone for a moment to allow the repeater to kick in. Then talk clearly and succinctly. Let go of the button to allow the dispatcher and other units to talk. Be sure to know which is the radio microphone and which is the public address (P.A.) mike.

And while we're at it, don't touch the radio to change the station or CD. Depending on departmental regulations, some officers with take home cars are able to install satellite radio, CDs, and other audio devices. The same goes for the in-car computer. This is their mobile office and they spend eight, ten, twelve plus hour shifts in this environment. They have preferences on how things are arranged and will not appreciate a visitor altering things without being requested to do so.

5) Eating Etiquette. Officers work hard and rely on each other in sometimes life-threatening situations. Eating on meal breaks is an important part of the culture of policing. Sitting at the table literally will give you an understanding of their world and their perspective.

Let the officers pick the eatery. You should eat prior to going on duty since you may have a high call volume shift and be unable to stop. If you and your host officer are able to take a break, the picked establishment may not be the type of food you would normally eat. Pick food off the menu wisely, so that you don't end up needing the officer to make a high speed run to a bathroom.

While many agencies have policies that prevent officers from accepting free or discounted food, it is not your place to discuss it at that point in public. If a discount is not extended to you as a civilian guest, you certainly should not pound your fist and demand that your bill be adjusted. On the contrary, if you are able to, I suggest you pick up the tab for the officers present in appreciation for them including you in their world. If the restaurant management insists on cutting the bill, you should leave a tip on the table that equals or exceeds the full-price check.

6) Less Talk, More Listen. Many folks when engaged in their first ride-along get quite excited. That leads to the motor mouth syndrome. Officers tend to be reserved when they first meet their ride-along. They are unsure of the person's motivations or perspective at first. It is better to go slow and allow the officer to get to know you. In an adaptation of the old adage, it is better to be quiet and listen than to speak and be thought of as a fool. It should without saying that profanity and other unprofessional speech has no place. These guidelines are particularly true of you are an aspiring officer

applying to the agency as they are checking you out as much as you are learning about them.

7) Confidentiality. Law enforcement officers see quite a bit of interesting stuff in their line of work. Even Hollywood can't make up what officers see in real-life. As a participant in a ride-along, you may see neighbors and other people from your community at their worst moment. Specifics and identifiers from the call are not for public consumption unless otherwise agreed upon. Some agencies may allow you to attend the pre-shift briefings. Again, information being discussed is not public in nature and you need to use discretion in discussing what you have seen and heard.

Notable exceptions pertain to the presence of credentialed media and news journalists who are approved for the ride-along with the full knowledge of their objective. Famous examples include the TV show "COPS."

On the local level, having a news crew onboard is a win-win situation. The department gets to showcase officers engaged in good policing and reach out to the community via the viewing audience. The TV station gets some great visuals that draw people to their newscasts especially during crucial ratings sweeps periods (that set advertiser rates).

As a police chief, I approved local network affiliates' news cameras to ride-along with patrol personnel in marked Ford Crown Victorias. We thoroughly discussed the rules and boundaries beforehand and each time it proved to be a rewarding experience for all concerned. These are folks who will reveal information publicly and have been approved to do so in advance by the nature of their mission.

8) Shotgun Release. Much like the radio, the officer may show you how to use the shotgun release in case events break bad and help from you is needed. Don't be like a certain ride-along that kept playing with the shotgun release during a call. Pushing the button and moving the shotgun repeatedly will make for a very nervous officer. It's best to trip the release only when you really and the officer really need you to do so.

9) No Weapons, Handcuffs. Unless you are a sworn officer from another agency who is allowed to have your police firearm and equipment with you, don't bring a gun, handcuffs, or the like on the ride-along. Most agencies have rules that prohibit such items even if you have a carry concealed weapon permit or license (CCW).

The only exception to the police equipment guidance offered is to wear a bullet resistant or ballistic vest. As a patrol division deputy sheriff, I had a spare vest in the trunk of my marked Chevrolet Caprice that I had ride-alongs wear. If you have your own, you may want to wear it hidden under your outer shirt.

10) Follow Instructions. The most important of the ten tips in this PoliceLink column is to follow the instructions of both the department and the host officer

or deputy sheriff. This is a major liability and responsibility for the agency and the officer.

Be aware that not all officers may be happy with your presence. Some police officers view their world as being closed to non-sworn folks, while others will welcome you with open arms. The law enforcer may or may not like ride-alongs.

Whether the officer volunteered or was volunteered by their supervisors certainly makes a difference in the quality of the ride-along experience. Even more crucial though is whether you listen to what you are supposed to do. Following instructions will go a long way towards creating good will.

For example, many agencies require that the ride-along stay in the car during calls for police service. If that is the case, do so unless the officer has you move for safety or other reasons.

Ask questions to clarify your limitations and instructions before you begin the adventure. If you fully understand your boundaries and follow instructions, your ride-along experience will be a terrific two-way bridge of understanding for you as a member of the community and for the law enforcer serving the community.

April 22, 2010
PoliceLink.com

10 Rules for Police Resumes

The hiring process used by law enforcement governmental entities differs quite a bit from the private sector. That divergence in process includes quantity and type of resumes. As a long-time criminal justice educator and former police chief, I have long counseled aspiring badge bearers on preparing their employment application packets in a bid to grab their coveted law enforcement agency slot.

Almost all governmental entities use an internally standardized application. These applications are designed with an eye towards public records and personnel hiring laws applicable in the jurisdiction, information that the police chief or sheriff is specifically wanting to ferret out, and materials to aid in the background investigation.

Increasingly, however, agencies are also asking for resumes. It is imperative you keep in mind these ten rules that are paramount to the agencies that will be reviewing your application.

1. Follow Directions

As with the application packet, if there are any instructions on what information and how to construct the resume, follow them. As a police chief, I wouldn't look at what answer the person put down, but how they did so. I did this because our law enforcement executives are under the belief that when you apply for a position you are at your most enthusiastic point in your career. This is the stage that you should be eager to cross every "t" and dot every "i". The presumption is that if you aren't that interested now, what will you be like in a year when you are off of Field Training Officer (FTO) status and out of probation?

For example, if the application directs that two copies of the resume be enclosed with no staple, but rather a paperclip in the top left corner, than that is how they should be included. If the resume instructions ask for dates in terms of month and year (MM/YYYY), than do that as well.

2. Be Detailed

Unless otherwise directed by the application packet instructions, error on the side of being too detailed. This is a major area that law enforcement resumes veer away from the overview approach of resumes used by the private sector. Similar to the style used by academia, the hiring authority in the policing world wants to have complete information. Information left out calls items into question. In our business, an omission is akin to a lie, so take the inclusion of all information seriously.

3. Be Truthful

"White lies" and other bending of the truth might be okay in the corporate world, but they don't fly in law enforcement. As I have explained to people, there are folks sitting in state prison because of my words in a courtroom. Those words, and everything else associated with law enforcement work, needs to be based on true facts. It is important for law enforcement executives to see a clear understanding of the need for truthfulness as evidenced by application materials including the resume.

Private sector managers expect to see certain jobs left off and only to see relevant employment history. Hiring agencies want to see all employers listed. They will want to see all schools and colleges attended.

4. Check Facts

Make sure that all that detailed information that you put down is in fact correct. You don't want to have out-dated or otherwise erroneous information on your law enforcement resume. Names, addresses and other information on previous employers is a common area where resume creators go wrong.

5. Check Spelling and Grammar

Because so much policing activity ends up in a report and in the courtroom, make sure to double-check your spelling and grammar. It's not wise to solely rely on the computerized spell check function. Sloppy paperwork is often used by legal counsel to attack your attention to detail and impugn your integrity and credibility. Remember, all the defense counsel has to do is introduce reasonable doubt into your criminal case. Police chiefs view your resume as an indicator of how you will handle the documentation surrounding legal cases.

6. Don't Sweat Length

In the private sector, much emphasis is placed on keeping the resume to one page; the omission of detail is often not important there. Since detail and truthfulness is an issue for law enforcement, unless otherwise directed by the agency's instructions, make the completeness of your resume the guiding principle; not the length. If goes for multiple pages, so be it.

7. Pick Font Wisely

Pick the type and size of font on your resume wisely. Since law enforcement is a traditional and conservative industry, you may want to keep to fonts such as Times New Roman or Arial. Fonts too large give an amateurish appearance, so size 12 is preferable. Others may be too small to be comfortably read.

8. Attention to Layout

Pay attention to your layout as well. Particularly since you don't have to jam it into one page, you can spread out the information and create lots of white empty space. That makes it easier to focus on the information in the respective section.

9. Bullet Point Information

Just because you have to include a lot of detail doesn't mean your resume needs to be unreadable. Use a bullet point style that can punctuate or highlight, in an easily digestible format, information that you want the reader to note. Long paragraphs tend to lose the reader's interest and blur, especially when read along with many other applicants' resumes.

10. Name and Contact Information

Make sure that you put your name and contact information at the top of the first sheet. Additionally, put your name at the top of each subsequent sheet in case the resume pages get separated. Triple-check that you have this information both accurate and in an easy place to locate.

Very importantly, as mentioned at the beginning of this article, follow any specific instructions that the hiring department gives you. Follow what they ask as that is a screening and elimination tool in and of itself. They may not even want a resume. Whatever the case, a resume, when requested, is another chance for you shine as brightly as the badge you want to wear.

May 28, 2010
PoliceLink.com

10 Ways to Generate Complaints on Patrol

With a public always looking to give law enforcement officers the benefit of the doubt and high profile police officers and deputy sheriffs never making mistakes that catch the public eye, this article is devoted to giving the aspiring and veteran law enforcer alike ten sure fire tips on how to generate complaints from the public and your supervisors. If you want to get attention from your agency's top administrators, be sure to pay close attention and adhere to these proven ways to garner the ire of the taxpayers.

Better yet, the truly devoted administrative complaint-generating officer may even aspire to the loftier criminal complaint level. At those heights, the payoff for a negative adjudication is having your room and board paid for by those same complaining taxpayers.

1) Keep your holster unsnapped and your hand on your gun at all times. You should ignore all the studies and experiments from my fellow firearms instructors. Just because they say that having the holster unsnapped at all times defeats the handgun retention advantages is no reason for you to do so. Ignore all those studies that show an officer that practices can draw and fire their weapon from a secured holster in an acceptable amount of time. By having your holster unsnapped and your hand on it, you'll be sure to create that adversarial relationship at every police-citizen contact you have during your shift.

2) Take your time getting to calls. Figuring that people think we in law enforcement take too long to get to calls for police service anyway, take your time. Make that complaint a good solid one by stopping for ice cream on the way. If you get held up on a higher priority call, be sure to tell dispatch not to contact the other caller and advise them that you will be enroute as soon as the exigent call is completed.

3) Use profanity. Lowering yourself to the level of street gangs and being disrespectful to the public will certainly irritate them. They will not view you as a professional or focus on the substance of what you are trying to tell them. Instead, they will fixate on your perceived disrespect and conjure up different ways to complain on you and otherwise damage your career.

4) Assault and Batter Suspects. Throw out all allegiance to the department's use of force policy and make yourself no better than the people we arrest. Be

sure to assault and batter suspects without provocation or justification. Better yet, be sure that those injuries are visible so that they can be photographed later and used against you to sustain the complaint.

5) Downgrade all Calls for Service. In the vein of being responsive to your bosses concerns on crime rates, be sure to artificially lower those local crime trends by reclassifying calls for service as you handle them. Make that assault a disorderly conduct and so on. For example, tell young men that if it is an assault, it meant that they were in fear so therefore they are chicken. Trick and browbeat people into changing the facts of the incident to meet the elements in lower crimes.

6) Smoke and eat at calls. When you do show up your calls for police service, be sure to smoke, eat, and engage in other such sloppy and unprofessional conduct. Don't worry about how such behavior appears or the role model influence that you have on young people.

7) Hassle Dispatchers. Ignore the conventional wisdom that dispatchers are your lifelines and hassle these folks no end. Be rude, demanding, and cut them off on the radio. You could even scratch the microphone with your nails to signal your unprofessional attitude. With the identifier technology embedded in today's communications equipment, the agency will be sure to be able to track down such behavior to you.

8) Mishandle Reports and Forget About Submitting Evidence and Crime Lab Items. Be sure that all of your

reports are incomplete, fraught with grammatical and spelling errors, and inaccurate. While you are at it, be sure to omit any written voluntary statements, any photographs, and use of force reports. Forget that the police are the world's biggest record keepers and that detailed, factual, chronologically reported documents are need for years to come for investigations, as well as the criminal and civil proceedings. And while you are at it, lose that evidence and forget to submit that evidence to the crime lab. Leave it in the trunk of your cruiser and ignore that chain of command evidence tag that is supposed to lead to your evidence custodian.

9) Shortcut calls. When you are at those pesky calls for service, be sure to ignore the need or requests to take fingerprints. Forget about canvassing the neighborhood for witnesses. Try to dispose of the call in the quickest possible so you can go on that coveted meal break.

10) Drive Fast. Be sure to drive fast, so you do not force drivers behind you to slow down. Fast driving, along with aggressive lane changing, are sure to garner attention. Most folks will assume that you are getting a pizza and not on the way to a call (even without your lights activated).

Theses ten items, while not all encompassing, are sure to generate complaints that you will have to answer. That may give you much desired time off during an administrative professional standards investigation to contemplate your new career and welcoming friends at the local car wash.

Better yet, some of those complaints may even lead to a separate criminal investigation and charges being pressed. Ignore that annoying idea that if we in criminal justice break the law, we're no better than them. Instead, focus on how much you'll enjoy meeting new friends and learning new activities when you get locked up for breaking the law.

On the other hand, if you want a long, productive, and rewarding record of respectfully generated service to the community, be sure to do the opposite of this negative list. There is some truth to the theory that active, professionally behaving officers do statistically generate more complaints. However, by acting in a diametrically opposed manner from the above, the incidences of complaints will be greatly minimized.

June 5, 2010
PoliceOne.com

Police to Professor: Making the Move to Academia

Many law enforcement officials fantasize of retiring to that dream job teaching in academia. They dream of working 20 hours a week with students who hang on their every word. Usually, that fantasy is set in a more temperate climate where the sun never sets. For many who pursue the ivory tower second career path, the cold wind of reality sets in as they turn in their application. This "Weinblatt's Tips" column focuses on how to get those positions and what to expect when you get there. For reasons of space, and since veteran law enforcers are most likely to migrate to two-year educational institutions, I'll confine the examination to teaching opportunities in community colleges.

Beyond the attractiveness of the perceived academic lifestyle, the real satisfaction for long-time educators like me is the realization that community college instructors are the Disneys of education. Community college professors help make dreams come true. I derive immense satisfaction, when contacted by students going back over a decade, from graduates who have turned their lives around. It is terrific to see that have evolved into successful law enforcers serving their communities. A good community college experience is part of that evolution.

And speaking of that envisioned lifestyle, while community college instructors do not have the pressure of the "publish or perish" time consuming research agenda present in many tenure track university settings, community colleges engender their own demands on faculty with an increased emphasis on teaching load. Not only are there more sections of classes to teach, the numbers of students in those classes is usually higher. That is particularly true these days with a struggling economy that causes community college enrollments to skyrocket. That said, community college professorships are plum jobs and the competition is fierce.

Teaching Options

Teaching opportunities for officers may take many forms. Officers could choose to bring their expertise to bear on the training side or they could share their experiences on the academic credit track. In addition to community colleges, they could work for a private training product oriented outfit, technical school, privately held college, or four-year bachelors and higher degree granting university.

With the advent of a booming on-line criminal justice oriented push in recent years, teaching at a distance has its attractive elements as well, though that primarily is an adjunct or part-time gig. Full-time teaching posts at community colleges, while they may require some on-line teaching load, the emphasis is still on the classroom teacher.

The instructional settings are varied and their applicability in your career plan depends on your interests, strength of resume, and your willingness to relocate. Government-run community colleges tend to have exclusivity in their service area, as they usually are part of a statewide, interconnected system.

Formulate a plan

Speaking of your career plan, you will need to plot out where you want to end up and what credential deficiencies you'll need to address to get to your goal. Take stock of where you are both in terms of your personal goals and your financial health. Most teaching gigs do not pay as well (at least initially) as high-ranking cop jobs. With a pension in hand, the switch to a lower paying teaching post becomes more realistic for many folks.

Next, you'll have to decide if you want to teach on the academic side of the house or train cadets in an academy setting and officers in advanced or specialized courses. Some educational institutions' criminal justice programs have the unusual luxury of wearing both hats (teaching in basic academy and advanced training, as well as criminal justice associates degree courses). Others have those separated under distinct academic and vocational or continuing education umbrellas. You may even consider higher-level academic posts that are primarily executive level, non-teaching posts in a director or dean level slot.

If your target is teaching in an academic setting, your educational accomplishments will have more weight. If your sites are set on training, your experience and instructor certifications will have greater emphasis for the hiring committee.

On the academic side, most institutions, particularly those that are regionally accredited, will look for you to possess a regionally accredited master's degree in criminal justice or a related field (criminology, law enforcement, corrections, public administration, etc.) or a master's degree in another area with an additional 18 graduate credit hours in criminal justice or a related field. There are six regional accrediting bodies in the United States and you are best served by having all of your college degrees under one of those "seals of approval." (Check out this site for more detailed information on regional accreditation, what it means, and the six accreditation organizations: http://distancelearn.about.com/od/accreditationinfo/a/re gional.htm)

Some places will allow you to teach academic courses with only a regionally accredited bachelor's degree in criminal justice or a related field along with relevant experiential requirements. It would behoove you to identify your target employer and find out what their requirements are so that you can earn the credentials prior to your application being filed with them.

If training is more your bag, you will need to take an instructor techniques course (or whatever your state's POST or criminal justice standards education and training honchos require). If your goal is to teach firearms or another high liability area such as vehicle operations, you may have to take additional instructor training courses.

After completing the train the trainer courses, many states require you to undergo an instructional internship and be evaluated by an experienced instructor and students prior to being granted state certification as a law enforcement instructor. Bear in mind that a few years down the road, your state may require you to show teaching time and proficiency in the training area in order for that state certification to be renewed.

Full-time jobs in the academic and training slots are few and far between. The competition is fierce especially in destination states such as Arizona, North Carolina, and Florida. Having been based in the Sunshine State for a number of years, I frequently get calls from officers, deputy sheriffs, and troopers across the nation (especially from snowy cities) who are looking for advice on how to move to Florida and teach criminal justice students.

Teaching experience

An important key to landing those coveted jobs is the ability to list teaching experience on your resume. Teaching a new entry technique at your agency's roll call is neat, but is not going to do the trick. Colleges are looking for substantial teaching experience in a comparable setting that they can understand.

A great way to garner that experience is to contact your local community college and pursue a part-time instructor slot. Being an adjunct is not a lifelong job, though some enjoy the stint for years. Rather, it is a way to fine tune your teaching skills and showcase your commitment to facilitating student learning and success.

Breaking in as an adjunct isn't easy though. For those that think that politics in policing is rough and tumble, let me point out that college politics can be brutal. Some academics have too much time on their hands and can obsess over petty jealousies and other issues. Having worked for community college criminal justice on a part-time or full-time basis in New Mexico, North Carolina, Florida, and Ohio, I can attest that there are some folks who will be like that everywhere.

Police vs. Academic Culture

Law enforcers that successfully make the transition from the police corporate culture to the academic arena do so by dropping their authoritative persona when interacting with the education folks. Serving as an adjunct instructor gives you the ability to learn how to interact with a liberal leaning group that has an outlook distinct from the conservative guys on the old shift.

Softening the edges of the rough and tumble police persona go a long way towards smoothing the transition from cop culture to academic arena. Such macho moves as wearing your gun exposed and spouting profanity may work well with the crew at the station, but it will elicit gasps of horror from a workforce that more readily gets their feathers ruffled.

Teaching at a community college does have some commonalities with the police world. Both involve interacting with diverse people and creating an inclusive environment where marginalization is kept to a minimum. And both deal with people at varying educational levels in a manner that is not condescending. Respect is a centerpiece of human relations for both endeavors.

Finding the jobs

Finding out about the full-time jobs is not that difficult. Publicly funded community colleges are bound by rules that dictate they advertise open full-time positions. The Chronicle of Higher Education has a jobs section that is rather complete. You may also check the higheredjobs.com, ccollegejobs.com and American Association of Community Colleges websites.

Part-time teaching posts are harder to discover. While your target college may advertise part-time faculty positions on their website, the web postings are usually out-dated and incomplete. Quite often, there is a full-time faculty or staff person in charge of academic and academy programs within a criminal justice department. Get to know that person. Share your area of expertise with him or her and be there for them when they get caught in an instructor-scheduling bind. You may even come in occasionally as a guest speaker until you can carve out your niche.

A typical breaking into the academic teaching arena scenario is involves a long-time instructor that gets sick or has other commitments that pull him or her away from the classroom. Be that "Johnny (or Joanna) on the spot" that will fill in and solve that educational manager's problem. Eventually, through your flexibility of schedule and helpful approach, you may find that you can claim "ownership" for that course or academy block of instruction.

Teaching in a community college can be a very rewarding pursuit. Many students hunger for those law enforcement veterans that can bring their real world experiences into the classroom to make academic theories come alive. Having been a professor and a manager over teachers, I believe that the most effective teachers are those that can balance thought-provoking academic theories with compelling real life experiences and war stories. That instructional blend, coupled with dynamic presentation skills, helps to excite and mold the next generation of enthusiastic, service-minded criminal justice professionals.

June 11, 2010
PoliceLink.com

You're In Trouble: Now What?

Most police officers and deputy sheriffs are honorable men and women trying to do a difficult job. I regularly deal with law enforcement issues that involve law enforcers in bad circumstances. Whether they are in fact responsible for an act involving intent or omission, many officers, particularly those at the beginning of their careers, are baffled by the process that most end up confronting at some point. This article covers a general overview and gives you some insight into what happens to the officer who "gets in trouble."

The policies and laws that govern personnel in law enforcement vary from agency to agency and state to state. Specific nuances of each area cannot be covered in this generalized article.

All officers end up having a complaint lodged against them at some point in their career. Some areas see more complaints while others appear to generate less. Officers who take certain steps can minimize the frequency of complaints lodged against them. That will be a future article. This PoliceLink.com article covers what to do if you get the dreaded call from the "Sarge."

Complaints usually are generated by misunderstandings of a police – civilian interaction. I have long said that we in policing are own worst enemies as we tend to miss opportunities to diplomatically explain what we are doing and why. That has often done the trick for me in my experience and I have observed that it does so for others as well.

That said there are times when either the officer actually handles a situation badly or the person complaining cannot be reasoned with. Whatever the case, the sequence of events begins with the original complaint.

Whether you are a newly minted or veteran officer (or an aspiring one targeting a particular agency to work for), "must reading" is the department's policies and procedures manual. That "bible" of the agency should be in writing and should reflect the status of current applicable statutes and case precedents, (you laugh, but quite a few "old school" administrators are not in touch with this concept).

While there is no national policy manual to govern the many local law enforcement agencies in the United States, laws, precedents, and past exemplary practices have helped to shape what are normal, standard of care parameters. The International Association of Chiefs of Police (IACP) and the Commission on Accreditation of Law Enforcement Agencies (CALEA) have formulated model policies that address many of the officer complaint issues.

Whatever the origin of your agency's policy book, that all-important document should clearly delineate what happens in the complaint process. It should be geared to treat the complaining party as well as the officer in a fair and impartial manner.

The first stop on the journey is usually the officer's supervisor. In some departments, uniformed patrol supervisors can handle the complaint, while more egregious allegations need to be forwarded up the chain of command or to the professional standards or internal affairs unit.

Your agency should treat all complaining parties with the respect and fairness you would hope would be afforded to your family members if they were to come forward with an allegation. Only by doing so, will the process be respected and the findings have credibility.

At this point, it should be readily apparent that any documentation you have concerning your actions is vital to your defense. Police reports should contain a tremendous amount of relevant (key word – relevant) detail. Police reports that are vague and lack important detail are not helpful in the criminal prosecution and can be damaging to you during any civil tort action taken against you and or your agency. Other types of evidence, such as patrol car dash cams, can go a long way towards quickly resolving a complaint.

For example, as a police chief, I received complaints of officer conduct during traffic stops. A review of the in-car video footage was all it took usually to get at the truth and exonerate the officer in question. A good administrator will examine all available evidence to be able to come to a fair and impartial determination.

Generally speaking, officers in heavily unionized departments, such as in the Northeast portion of the United States, are afforded a little more protection. Officers in right to work states, such as in the Southeast, have less recourse. In the Southeast, many of the elected sheriffs, as ruled by the courts in North Carolina, have more ability to discipline and terminate their deputies, who are serving at will, than police chiefs do with municipal police officers.

Depending on the severity of the allegation and the supervisory staff's preliminary determination of that misconduct's probability of occurrence, the employee may be suspended with or without pay pending further investigation.

If the agency is following an accepted standard of internal investigation procedures, the accused officer will have the right to have the accusation or complaint shown to him or her in written form. The officer would also be interviewed at a reasonable hour or within their normal working hours, as well as be afforded reasonable breaks during the interview.

Departments generally go with a standard that has been backed up by court decisions such as U.S. Supreme Court cases Garrity v. New Jersey, (1967) and, for the feds, Kalkines v. United States, (1973). Officers under an administrative investigation can refuse to answer questions. This is really applicable if there is the belief that a criminal component could arise. However, refusing to answer questions may form the evidentiary basis for charges. Officers, like other governmental workers, can be compelled to answer within an administrative context, as that is a condition of employment.

It is important in this process is that the department should also explain that this is an administrative process and that any criminal charges that could arise from the officer's acts or omissions are to be handled separately from the internal affairs investigation. Those matters should be referred to an appropriate criminal investigation unit or, better yet to avoid the appearance of a conflict of interest, another agency. The idea here is that the employee should not be forced to choose between his or her constitutionally protected Fifth Amendment right against self-incrimination (think Miranda v. Arizona) and his or her job.

The Garrity Warning should be in writing. Some agencies issue it and have the target officer sign it as a matter of course. Others do so only when they feel there is a good chance that a criminal component may arise out of the officer's conduct. Importantly, false statements are not protected against criminal prosecution during any part of the investigation.

Most agencies will not allow legal counsel during the administrative investigation interview. Some will, however, allow you to have a non-involved supervisor present. Others, particularly in the Northeast, will allow you to have a union representative accompany the officer. Agencies tend to audiotape or videotape the interview.

Be aware that property owned by the employing governmental entity is subject to search. Unless otherwise restricted by local protocol, most agencies can search your departmentally issued equipment including the patrol car, locker, and computer.

Following the conclusion of the investigation, findings and recommendations are made and forwarded up the chain of command with one of the four (or similar) following dispositions:

1) Sustained: The officer did as the allegation said.
2) Not Sustained: The allegation could not be proven or unproven
3) Unfounded: The allegation is false. The officer wasn't present during the allegation or the actions did not occur.
4) Exonerated: The officer did the act or omission alleged, but that it did not constitute a violation of policy.

Most agencies will provide a written copy of the findings to the officer, as well as to the originator of the complaint. The disposition also tends to make its way for a period of time into performance reviews, as well as to specialized assignment transfer requests.

Employees in a probationary employment status with a finding of sustained are particularly vulnerable during the disciplinary phase as their protections are few, if any. In most places, there is little recourse as a probationary officer can be terminated at any time during that probationary period. Probation is normally pegged at one year, although there are a few departments where it can run for two years. It can also be extended under remedial or disciplinary instances.

If it is sustained and the employee is terminated, he or she (if off probation) usually has the ability within a certain timeframe to appeal or grieve the matter to a neutral party such as the civil service board or the city manager.

If the sustained allegation results in a suspension, departments usually have guidelines as to how that suspension is served. For example, with a smaller suspension punishment, the employee may be able to use accrued vacation time to settle the matter. For longer periods, they may be able to only utilize half.

Some departments will send the employee to remedial training. This is seen quite a bit for officers who are involved in on-duty vehicle crashes who are sent to driver training. Officers who use inappropriate language are often enrolled in human diversity or sensitivity training.

Being in trouble is no fun either as a teenager or an adult law enforcer. The key difference for the officer or deputy sheriff is to remain calm and be professional in the face of the allegation. Emotional or irrational actions will only lend credibility to any complaint and not help the search for the truth or your service to the community.

June 27, 2010
Examiner.com

Reality TV show cop Betsy Brantner Smith: "women police have come far"

Betsy Brantner Smith started in law enforcement some three decades ago; although you wouldn't think so given the vitality and energy she brings to her endeavors. And while women in policing have come a long way during the years she discharged the duties of a demanding profession, the woman who retired a year ago at the rank of sergeant, enjoyed the challenges even back then and excelled in spite of them.

"I couldn't believe that they paid me to do this," said Brantner Smith, otherwise known as The Sarge, recently on The Cop Doc radio show. "I loved being a police officer.

Female Forces

Known to many for her starring role in The Biography Channel's unscripted police reality show "Female Forces" (http://www.biography.com/female-forces/), Brantner Smith has gotten used to her high profile, jet-setting life signing autographs. The former Naperville, IL, Police sergeant has turned her part-time speaking, teaching, and writing stints into a full-time, high profile gig.

"People recognize me and I think the show helped women, and men, see female officers in a positive way," Brantner Smith said. "It's important not to lump all of the women on the show together. While we all enjoyed it, we got different things out of our participation."

Roy Bedard, a long-time police officer himself, produced "Female Forces" and has worked with Brantner Smith on a variety of projects. The police trainer and man behind RRB Systems said that Brantner Smith is a great officer and he enjoyed working with her. "Female officers can be feminine and still be great warriors," Bedard said. "That's one of the great qualities that Betsy has. She can fight."

Brantner Smith said that she tells women who attend her well-respected Caliber Press Street Survival Seminar for Women, where she is the lead instructor, that they can be a professional law enforcer and still be woman. "They don't have to sacrifice their femininity," she explained detailing how many young women entering into the field think they have to be tougher than the men. "What I tell them is we're not men. We are women and that is ok."

The Street Survival Seminar for Women lead instructor duties are but one way she has parlayed her talents into a cottage industry of law enforcement expertise. She has become synonymous with the breaking of expectations as she crashed through the glass ceiling of law enforcement.

The Sarge's Career

Her career as a sworn law enforcer has had a varied path and that's given her much to draw from as she dispenses wisdom to a new generation of serving and aspiring law enforcers. Among her titles in addition to patrol officer: K-9 unit supervisor, field training sergeant, receruitment team sergeant, crowd control and bike patrol coordinator, and supervisor of the community education and crime prevention unit.

Each slot brought with it unique challenges and learning opportunities that helped Brantner Smith to spread her wings. Some colleagues embraced her presence, while others didn't. Still others went out of their way to sabotage her career.

"I got write ups that we laugh about now, but back then were hard. One was for standing with my legs too far apart for a woman," Brantner Smith recalled. Women are biologically different and it's hard for us not to cry." She said that she struggled at times not to cry in front of the guys.

Brantner Smith credits a progressive police chief, long since passed away, who was ahead of his time for mentoring and encouraging her in her career. Mentors are an important part of the assimilation and success of women in policing, according to Brantner Smith.

The Sarge has expanded beyond just her squad of officers and now finds herself in the role of coach for women all across the United States. She meets many of them in her courses or through her writings. "Women have a moral duty to mentor other women and help them to be successful," she said.

"Women were often thought of as entering the business just to find themselves a husband," she added. "She explained that many officers end up marrying other law enforcers, or people in the helping professions such as nurses. Relationships suffer for many women due to the pressures of the job.

Marriage is yet another area where Brantner Smith has excelled, although she concedes it took her sometime to find the right relationship. Dave Smith, a retired Arizona Highway Patrol lieutenant who is well-known for his creation in 1980 of the "J.D. Buck Savage" police training video character, is the male half of a unique partnership. Together they operate the Chicago area based Dave Smith & Associates. Smith, an instructor for Caliber Press Street Survival, as well as a columnist for PoliceOne.com and Police Magazine, is quick to give credit and attention to the training acumen of his wife.

On the other hand, as you would hope for in a symbiotic relationship like marriage, Betsy Brantner Smith is quick to toot the horn of Buck Savage. In that supportive vein, she enthusiastically encouraged the mention of Smith's recently authored book, "In My Sights."

As for Branter Smith and her penning of wisdom from the police training realm, she too keeps busy with a computer never far from her fingertips. She has regular columns for PoliceOne.com and PoliceLink.com. It seems that much of her writing ability stems, like a lot of writers, from her affinity for reading. "I tell women all the time that they need to read. In our training courses, we distribute a reading list." A favorite read of hers right now that she's encouraging her legions of followers to buy: Michael Gurian's "Leadership and the Sexes."

Brantner Smith may have retired a year ago after 29 years of serving her community, but the service mentality and its energetic delivery hasn't stopped. These days, the Sarge's beat has been expanded across all jurisdictional boundaries and is geared towards assisting the aspirations, as well as the very survival, of law enforcement learners.

Appendix

Partial Listing of Published Articles by
Dr. Richard Weinblatt

Examiner.com June 30, 2010
"Policing the Twilight, Drake and Justin Bieber beats"

Examiner.com June 30, 2010
"Why police should suspect missing Kyron Horman's stepmom"

Examiner.com June 27, 2010
"Police shift tactics at G20 Global Economic Summit in Toronto"

Examiner.com June 27, 2010
"Reality TV show cop Betsy Brantner Smith: women police have come far"

Examiner.com June 27, 2010
"Detroit Police: proud of crime stat. murder rate drop"
Examiner.com June 24, 2010
"Experts question Joran van der Sloot's police blame game"

PoliceLink.com June 11, 2010
"You're In Trouble: Now What?"

PoliceOne.com June 5, 2010
"Police to Professor: Making the Move to Academia"

PoliceLink.com May 28, 2010
"10 Ways to Generate Complaints on Patrol"

PoliceLink.com April 22, 2010
"10 Rules for Police Resumes"

PoliceLink.com April 6, 2010
"10 Tips for Ride-Alongs"

PoliceLink.com March 11, 2010
"10 Tricks for Picking the Right Department"
Newark Advocate (OH) & NewarkAdvocate.com
January 15, 2010
"Police Academy Students Pursuing their Dreams"

PoliceLink.com October 15, 2009
"The Bottom Line of Seat Belts for Law Enforcers"

PoliceLink.com October 1, 2009
"10 Domestic Violence Reminders for Veteran
Officers"

PoliceLink.com September 2009
"Ten Tips for On Target Academy Firearms Training"

PoliceOne.com August 25, 2009
Weinblatt's Tips column: "Top 10 social networking
tips for cops"

PoliceOne.com August 3, 2009
Weinblatt's Tip column: "There's a New Sheriff in this
Media Town"

CNN AC360 Anderson Cooper blog (guest writer on Anderson Cooper's CNN.com blog) - July 30, 2009
"Gates, Crowley and The President: Calling it how I see it"

PoliceLink.com July 24, 2009
"Response to National Racial Debate: Gates, Crowley and the President"

PoliceLink.com January 2009
"Bad Credit, Bad Applicant"
Domestic Preparedness Journal September 10, 2008
"When Disaster Strikes: Gaining Peace of Mind"

PoliceLink.com August 25, 2008
"Professionalism: What Does Your Badge Stand For?"

PoliceOne.com August 22, 2008
Weinblatt's Tips column: "P1 Exclusive: What law enforcement can learn from the Caylee Anthony case"

PoliceLink.com August 2008
"Answering Common Oral Hiring Board Questions"

PoliceLink.com July 2008
"10 Tips for Mastering the Police Oral Board"

PoliceOne.com May 16, 2008
"National Police Week: Reflecting on our vulnerabilities"

PoliceLink.com April 2008
"Getting Serious About Joining the Force"

PoliceLink.com November 26, 2007
"Ten Tips for Dealing with the Opposite Sex"

PoliceLink.com November 20, 2007
"Surviving Your Prisoner Transport"

PoliceOne.com November 16, 2007
Weinblatt's Tips column: "10 Taser tips for LEOs"

PoliceLink.com October 30, 2007
"Promotions: The Courses That Count"

PoliceLink.com July 2, 2007
"So you wanna be a cop… First impressions count!"

PoliceOne.com April 20, 2007
Weinblatt's Tips column: "Tips for major incident media relations in the wake of the Virginia Tech shooting"

PoliceOne.com February 16, 2007
Weinblatt's Tips column: "10 tips for officers engaged in off-duty incidents"

PoliceOne.com March 6, 2006
Weinblatt's Tips column: "PoliceOne Exclusive: Domestic disturbance response: 10 tips for winning at these volatile calls"

Officer.com March 6, 2006
Reserve Power column: "The Flip Side: Why Some
Reserves Hate Cops"

Officer.com February 17, 2006
Career Corner column: "How to Keep Your Boss
Happy: How to acquire power in the agency"

Officer.com February 6, 2006
Reserve Power column: "Why Some Cops Hate
Reserves: A crack in the police family"

PoliceOne.com January 16, 2006
The Police and the Press column: "Press releases: Used
and abused"

Officer.com January 16, 2006
Career Corner column: "Inside the FBI National
Academy: The FBI NA and Others are Key to
Promotion"

PoliceOne.com January 4, 2006
Weinblatt's Tips column: "Police officer suicide
prevention: Officers kill themselves at higher rate than
general population"

PoliceOne.com January 3, 2006
Weinblatt's Tips column: "PoliceOne members
respond"

Officer.com January 3, 2006
Reserve Power column: "The Ultimate Sacrifice: Line of Duty Deaths Underscore Officers' Service"

Officer.com December 16, 2005
Career Corner column: "Academic Jobs for the Cop: How to Land those Teaching Gigs"

PoliceOne.com December 14, 2005
Weinblatt's Tips column: "Creative cuffing for small-wristed subjects"

Officer.com November 22, 2005
Reserve Power column: "The Original Homeland Security Force: For volunteer cops, it's the same old 'thang'"

PoliceOne.com November 21, 2005
Weinblatt's Tips column: "10 tips for talking with kids"

PoliceOne.com November 10, 2005
Weinblatt's Tips column: "Searching for a clue"

PoliceOne.com November 10, 2005
Weinblatt's Tip column: "Death notifications: A tough police assignment"

PoliceOne.com November 10, 2005
Weinblatt's Tips column: "Carrying a knife: Officer safety and administrative considerations"

PoliceOne.com November 10, 2005
Weinblatt's Tips column: "10 ways to minimize complaints"

PoliceOne.com November 10, 2005
Weinblatt's Tip column: "Firearms training: train like you play"

PoliceOne.com November 10, 2005
Weinblatt's Tips column: "Crime scenes: stopping the evidence eradication gremlins"

PoliceOne.com October 26, 2005
Tip: "Returning DL can help avoid consent problems"

The Orlando Sentinel (daily newspaper Orlando, Florida) October 19, 2005
Editorial: "A rip in fabric that holds law enforcement together"

PoliceOne.com October 19, 2005
The Police and the Press column: "The absence of a police marketing mentality"

Officer.com October 19, 2005
Career Corner column: "The Good, the Bad, and the Ugly of Online College Degrees"

PoliceOne.com October 12, 2005
Officer Safety Tip: "Officer safety: It's not just an on-duty thing"

PoliceOne.com October 3, 2005
Training Tip: "AlcoSensor breath samples: How to tell if your subject is cooperating"

PoliceOne.com September 26, 2005
Officer Safety Tip: "The forgotten piece of equipment: handcuffs"

PoliceOne.com September 19, 2005
Officer Safety Tip & Training Tip: "Intersection safety for backup units"

PoliceOne.com August 30, 2005
The Police and the Press column: "Putting a human face on the police: Making an emotional connection"

PoliceOne.com May 24, 2005
The Police and the Press column: "P1 Exclusive: Ten Tips for Working with the Media"

PoliceOne.com April 4, 2005
The Police and the Press column: "How History Makes the Future of Police Media Relations Clearer"

PoliceOne.com April 28, 2004
The Police and the Press column: "The Image in the Mirror: The Enemy has a Face"

The Courier-Tribune (daily newspaper Asheboro, North Carolina) Friday, April 23, 2004 Guest Column: "Appreciation for a job well done"

American Police Beat April 2004
"How to give yourself a good shot at the job: Don't shoot yourself in the foot before you even get to the interview"

The Courier-Tribune (daily newspaper Asheboro, North Carolina) Sunday, January 4, 2004
Guest Column: "Understanding your partnership with your police"

Sheriff Magazine January-February 2003
"Sheriffs' Psychologists: The Ultimate Backup for the Progressive Sheriff's Office"

Law and Order: The Magazine for Police Management May 2001
"Alaska's Reserves Brave the Elements"

Law and Order: The Magazine for Police Management May 2000
"Departmental Gyms Become Fitness Rooms: Final Phase in a Holistic Fitness Approach"

Law and Order: The Magazine for Police Management May 2000
"Beyond Hurricanes: Riots, Bombings are 21st Century Reserve Duties"

Law and Order: The Magazine for Police Management April 2000
"Solving High Tech Crimes: Private and Public Sector Partnerships"

Corrections Technology Management Magazine
March/April 2000
"Role-Playing"

Law and Order: The Magazine for Police Management
February 2000
"Creative Funding Makes AEDs a Reality in Patrol
Cars"

Law and Order: The Magazine for Police Management
January 2000
"Volunteers Assist in Private/Public Sector Partnership

Law and Order: The Magazine for Police Management
December 1999
"The Paramilitary vs. Academic Training Debate"

Law and Order: The Magazine for Police Management
December 1999
"Managing Off-Duty Jobs: A Clear Policy Is The Key
To Success"

Corrections Technology and Management Magazine
November/December 1999
"So You Want To Be a Volunteer Probation Officer"

Law and Order: The Magazine for Police Management
November 1999
"Bridging Gaps in Assignments: Villa Park Fills in with
Auxiliary and Part-time Officers"

Law and Order: The Magazine for Police Management
October 1999
"IACP Conference 1999: Charlotte: The Queen City"

Law and Order: The Magazine for Police Management
October 1999
"Charlotte-Mecklenburg Police: 21st Century
Technology and Community Service"

Law and Order: The Magazine for Police Management
October 1999
"The Shifting Landscape of Chief Jobs: What's Changed
and How to Forge a Path"

Law and Order: The Magazine for Police Management
September 1999
"Agencies Look to Year 2000: Assess Y2K Options"

Law and Order: The Magazine for Police Management
September 1999
"Volunteer SPCA Officers: Working with Local Police
to Protect Animals"

Law and Order: The Magazine for Police Management
August 1999 "Special Report: New Training Concept:
New Police Training Philosophy: Adult Learning Model
on Verge of Nationwide Rollout"

Law and Order: The Magazine for Police Management
August 1999 "RCMP Takes Learning to the Streets"

Law and Order: The Magazine for Police Management
August 1999
"The Evolution of Police Footwear: It is the Era of Air
Jordans and Bloodborne Pathogens"

Law and Order: The Magazine for Police Management
May 1999
"Discovering a Valuable Asset: Reserve Search and
Rescue Units"

Corrections Technology Management Magazine
October 1998
"Come Fly With Me: Feds Take to the Air to Help
Locals with Safe, Economical Inmate Moves"

Corrections Technology Management Magazine
May/June 1998
"Point-Counterpoint: Weighing in on Privatization"

Law and Order: The Magazine for Police Management
May 1998
"Changing the Corporate Culture: How One State
Agency Took on the Challenge"

Corrections Technology Management Magazine March
1998
"Locals Get A Piece of the Action from Uncle Sam:
Strapped Jails Turn Finances Around: Facilities Garner
Federal Prisoners and Dollars"

Law and Order: The Magazine for Police Management
February 1998
"Reserve Expertise Makes Air Support A Reality"

Corrections Technology Management Magazine
February 1998
"Point-Counterpoint: Showdown in the Arizona Desert:
Maricopa County's Tent City Jail"

Law and Order: The Magazine for Police Management
December 1997
"Negative Perceptions Common: Regulars Question
Value of Reserves"

Police: The Law Enforcement Magazine October 1997
So You Wanna' Be a Police Chief: Aspiring to the Top
Rank of Law Enforcement Today Takes More
Experience, Training, Education, Skills, and Political
Savvy Than Ever Before"

Law and Order: The Magazine for Police Management
September 1997
"Academies Put Civilians in the Shotgun Seat: Law
Enforcement Takes Community Policing to the Next
Level"

American Police Beat June 1997
"Is The Grass Greener at the Aurora, Colorado Police
Department?"

Law and Order: The Magazine for Law Enforcement
Management June 1997
"Riding with Reserve FTOs: Field Training Programs
Vary in Different Departments for Reserve Officer
Recruits"

Sheriff Magazine March-April 1997
"Sheriffs Take on Rural Patrol Challenge"

Law and Order: The Magazine for Police Management
April 1997
"Special Report: Bicycles: More Than Just a Balancing
Act"

Law and Order: The Magazine for Police Management
April 1997
"Rank Insignia for Reserves: Debate Revolves Around
Public Perception and Officer Acceptance"

American Police Beat March 1997
"The Paychecks are High and So Is Morale"

Law and Order: The Magazine for Police Management
March 1997
"Special Report: S.W.A.T.: Counseling and Support for
S.W.A.T. Personnel"

Sheriff Magazine January-February 1997
"Sheriffs Find Innovative Solutions: Providing Jail
Medical Services with Limited Funds"

Law and Order: The Magazine for Police Management
December 1996
"Advice for Reserves: The Reserves' Legal Eagles and
Insurance Icons Weigh In"

Police: The Law Officer's Magazine October 1996
"Have Gun, Will Travel: Gaining Certification in the
New Frontier"

Law and Order: The Magazine for Police Management
September 1996
"Reserve Duties Vary in the Bay State: Massachusetts
Officers Wear Many Hats"

Law and Order: The Magazine for Police Management
April 1996
"Reserve Officers Man Boats: Turnover is Low for
Police on the 'Baywatch' Beat"

Law and Order: The Magazine for Police Management
March 1996
"Reserves Patrol on Bicycles: This New Breed is
Cutting a Wide Path as they Pedal Forth"

Law and Order: The Magazine for Police Management
November 1995
"Take-Home Cars for Reserves: Officer Effectiveness
and Community Presence Enhanced by Program"

Law and Order: The Magazine for Police Management
August 1995
"A Class Act: University Police Reserves Pass the Test
of Professionalism"

Law and Order: The Magazine for Police Management
April 1995
"N. Carolina Reserves Among Top Ranked: Volunteers
Find the Sweat and Hard Work are Worth It"

Law and Order: The Magazine for Police Management
February 1995
"P.E.P. Program: Part-Time Officer Training in Illinois"

Law and Order: The Magazine for Police Management
December 1994
"Liaison Officers: A Vital Link in a Reserve Operation"

Law and Order: The Magazine for Police Management
September 1994
"Oral Boards Go High-Tech"

Law and Order: The Magazine for Police Management
August 1994
"Police Footwear Meets the 'Reebok Generation'"

Law and Order: The Magazine for Police Management
August 1994
"Battle Dress Utility"

Law and Order: The Magazine for Police Management
June 1994
"Seasonal Reserves: Part-time Paid Personnel Fill in the Gaps"

Law and Order: The Magazine for Police Management
April 1994
"Reserves, Regulars and Regulators: How They Work Together in New Mexico"

The Narc Officer March/April 1994
"Reserve Heroes"

Law and Order: The Magazine for Police Management
February 1994
"Reserves Mount Up: Provide Services Otherwise Curtailed"

Law and Order: The Magazine for Police Management
December 1993
"Professionalism Reduces Liability: Trained Reserves
Make Positive Contribution"

Law and Order: The Magazine for Police Management
October 1993
"Reserves Excel in the Sunshine State: Training
Exceeds Standards"

Law and Order: The Magazine for Police Management
August 1993
"Reserve Data Available: New Book Provides
Everything You'll Want to Know"

Police: The Law Officer's Magazine July 1993
"Credence & Credibility: Training, Selection Standards,
and Liability Still Top The List of Concerns About
Reserve Officers. Increased Professionalism, However,
Has Brought Increased Respect"

Law and Order: The Magazine for Police Management
June 1993
"Reserve Motorcycles: A Positive Public Relations
Impact"

21st Century Policing Summer 1993
"Volunteer Officers and Community Policing"

Law and Order: The Magazine for Police Management
April 1993
"Reserve Detectives"

The F.O.P. Journal Spring/Summer 1993
"Reserve Policing: Stepping Stone to a Career"

Law and Order: The Magazine for Police Management
February 1993
"'Freelance' Reserves"

Law and Order: The Magazine for Police Management
December 1992
"Reserve Wildlife Officers: A Different Breed"

Law and Order: The Magazine for Police Management
October 1992
"Reserve K-9"

Law and Order: The Magazine for Police Management
August 1992
"The Thin Line Between Reserve and Full Time"

Law and Order: The Magazine for Police Management
April 1992
"Alabama Reserves Alive and Well"

Law and Order: The Magazine for Police Management
February 1992
"The Police and The Media"

Law and Order: The Magazine for Police Management
February 1992
"The Golden State of California Reserves"

Law and Order: The Magazine for Police Management
December 1991
"The Birth of a Volunteer Officer Program"

The Police Investigator October 1991
"Hostage Incidents: The Experts Respond"

Law and Order: The Magazine for Police Management
October 1991
"The State of the State Reserve Trooper"

Law and Order: The Magazine for Police Management
September 1991
"Accreditation: A Force Affecting Reserve Officers"

The TMPA Quarterly July 1991
"Texas Reserve Cops: The Lone Star State is Pioneering
the Way"

The Narc Officer February 1991
"The Use of Reserve Officers in the War on Drugs"

The Reserve Law Officer 4th Quarter 1990
"Does TV Depict 'Real Life' Police Work?"

www.ingramcontent.com/pod-product-compliance
Lightning Source LLC
Chambersburg PA
CBHW060846280326
41934CB00007B/938